VOICES FROM THE PAST

An Autobiography of a London Cypriot

By Fotis Loizou

Copyright © Fotis Loizou 2011

This book is sold subject to the condition that it shall not,
by way of trade otherwise, be lent, resold, hired out, or otherwise circulated
without the publisher's prior consent in any form of binding or cover other than
that in which it is published and without a similar condition, including this
condition, being imposed on the subsequent purchaser.

Fotis Loizou asserts the moral right to
be identified as the author of this work.

Publisher F. Loizou
Email: loizou@valeriya.orangehome.co.uk

This book is available in the British Library.

ISBN 978-0-9570975-0-6

Cover design : Fotis Loizou

For my mother and father

MOTHER

My mother awoke before the birds
had sung their mornings melodies.
She awoke in the early morning darkness
with the star of dawn still
flickering in the falling night sky
while in motionless early morning,
deep, sweet sleep as if from carved cool marble,
we dreamed.
She dressed quickly
in her coarse skirt
and plain blouse.
On her feet she put on a pair of worn shoes.
She then bathed her face
In clean, cold, refreshing water,
combed her silky, fine, straight, black hair:
she could have been an actress
or a celebrity in another place,
in another time.
She saw no need for make up
in her present circumstances.
Everything was a stark reality
like the morning sun
that peeped over the dark horizon.
She had no young woman's fantasies
for the Parisian or London look
that she had once glimpsed
in a fashion magazine,
in a house that she cleaned,
scrubbed and polished,
where the skin on her hands grew rough
and her finger nails splintered.
A piece of bread,
a cup of water
was her morning sustenance.
At the *baranga** door

she looked back at us
before stepping out
- a silent silhouette
against a morning, orange sky.

~

Mother was working for English service families at 'Four Miles'. She cleaned their houses from morning until night. I was hardly more than an infant and she would leave me at home to be looked after by my sister who was only a child herself. The 1950s was a time of economic hardship in Cyprus and father had already gone abroad to seek some solution to the economic deprivations that confronted us. He and thousands of other Cypriots, who left Cyprus at that time, were in search of a better life; mother was left behind to work and to bring up my sister and me.

How hard her life must have been! It seems that most mothers, no matter where they are, face the same problem of who is to look after the children to enable them to work. My mother thought that she had discovered the perfect solution to the problem. She enrolled me at a newly opened nursery. She had a lot of pride and wanted to do things independently, not to ask for help from her relatives. So she worked harder, cleaned two or three houses more every day. She worked without pause from morning until night. They paid her a few shillings for her labour, unable to believe how cheap all that mundane work was that they would have to have done themselves in their terraced and semis back in England. She worked very hard so she could pay for the nursery fee, to feed and to clothe us. She wanted us to be as good as anybody else but she had to earn that privilege with the sweat of her brow.

On one particular day she tried to do more than she could handle in the given time, she was late for the bus that would have enabled her to collect me on time from the nursery. I remember that day like a dream. All the children had been collected by their parents and I was left alone with the sombre family who were the nursery proprietors. They sat waiting without speaking and even though I was only four or five years old I sensed that they were in some way very annoyed and so I played silently without daring to look up at their stern faces.

At long last my mother arrived. I ran to her as if she was my liberator. She hardly spoke to me. She immediately addressed the proprietor in an apologetic voice.

"I am sorry, Mr. Nicholas. I had so much work... and I missed my bus..."

Mr. Nicholas had a fat, perspiring face with a small, spiky moustache. He spoke in a very quiet and serious manner as if he was a doctor with bad news.

"Mrs. Loizou, you are not late by only a few minutes but by more than an hour."

His voice rose to a higher note on the last syllable as if to add emphasis to what he was saying.

"I can see," he continued, "it is going to be a problem getting here on time to collect your child and this is very difficult for us because we are tired and we have other things to do."

He looked a little embarrassed at having to play the role of a harder person than what he actually was and nervously glanced at his little wife who was sitting tense and silent on one side of the porch, observing the unfolding events. My mother was not prepared to change her plans just yet and insisted on the agreed arrangement. Despite her tiredness she found the strength to at least try some negotiation. She was not one to walk away from a challenge.

"Mr. Nicholas, I have only been this late just this one time and I promise you it will not happen again. It was unforeseen, the lady who

I work for on this day had some very important unexpected guests and she pleaded with me to stay an extra two hours for double the hourly rate...I can give you some extra money for the additional hour that my child has been with you."

She then started to desperately search her hand bag for the money that she had received on that day, took out some notes and thrust them at Mr. Nicholas who raised his palms as if to defend himself. He spoke quietly but firmly while his little wife now standing behind him looked very annoyed, indeed.

"No, Mrs. Loizou, this is not about money but it is about being able to pick up your child on time. I also have to think of the other people who work with me because they need to be released from their duties after a long working day. I am sorry ....I also sometimes have a tight schedule and I depend on the parents picking up their children on time. You just haven't been able to do that."

By the end of his little speech he was perspiring profusely and mother realised that Mr. Nicholas was not going to be allowed to change his mind.

Without saying another word, mother took me by the hand and we both walked out of the nursery. Soon after, mother cancelled my place at the nursery and she decided to ask grandmother to look after me. She wanted me to attend the nursery but it seemed there were too many obstacles in the way.

~

We travelled by bus from Varosi* where we lived in a *baranga*, a type of wooden house, near the sea front. We caught the bus from the bus station in the centre of town. As soon as we boarded the bus we began to immediately perspire. It felt hot and airless like an oven.

Despite this the bus soon filled with people from the village who had been conducting their business in town and were now in a hurry to return home before the intense heat of the early afternoon. There were three or four students from the Varosi gymnasium, the main secondary school of the town, who were easily recognizable by their peaked military style high school caps and who, despite the heat, were engaged in animated discussion. Some village house wives sat at the rear of the bus. They had probably attended to various essential matters in town or perhaps had been shopping for some items that couldn't be found in the village shop. They talked quietly amongst themselves and sometimes modest laughter could be heard coming from them. Some other people sat alone without speaking with anyone, waiting patiently, sometimes with closed eyes, for the bus journey to begin.

The bus driver, a big, middle aged man with a pot belly, eventually took his seat and with a turn of the ignition key the old engine of the ancient bus made a great rusty noise, grumbled and grunted into reluctant motion. The tired, old bus began to make its way slowly through the narrow streets of Varosi; we passed by the broad and bulky Venetian walls* that had successfully defended the city from the Ottoman siege in the 16th century until the defenders were forced by hunger and starvation to surrender to the invaders. Behind them now lived the Turkish Cypriot citizens of Famagusta who only reluctantly venture beyond their protection. The demand for Enosis, union with Greece, by the Greek Cypriots was rapidly becoming a serious crisis. The old bus slowly accelerated, moving beyond the shadow of the city walls and into the open countryside.

We journeyed from the town to the village on a day of bright, cutting sunshine and cloudless blue skies. The burning heat drained our energy; it was intense and oppressive, making our bodies feel heavy and sleepy. The animated discussion of the gymnasium students gradually lost its intensity and then fizzled out. The house wives in the rear had stopped talking and each one of them was now immersed in her own private thoughts. The passengers, who sat alone, had either fallen asleep or were gazing aimlessly out of the window. With each passing mile, our journey grew in discomfort. We passed through a landscape of sun scorched grass dotted here and there with wrinkled olive trees. Occasionally, we glimpsed some isolated figures, working in the fields. They seemed tiny on a huge landscape, working under a clear blue sky, relentlessly being beaten by a harsh, merciless summer sun.

The scene could have been from a thousand years ago; it was the timeless engagement of men toiling to bring forth fruit from the soil. When our bus drew parallel with them, the figures on the landscape looked up and waved as the old bus trundled along the uneven road, churning clouds of dust in its wake.

Eventually, the bus stopped outside the Stylloi *café, in the centre of the tiny village which was no more then a cluster of white washed houses built around a few narrow streets that seemed particularly isolated during the heat of the day.

Grandmother's house was just a short walk from the stop. It was a house built of *plythari*,* a brick made from mud and straw, a technique that must have somehow been handed down from the time of the Pharaohs in Egypt. The white washed house had belonged to my grandfather and his first wife. When she had passed away my grandfather eventually remarried and continued to live in the same house with his new wife, my grandmother Kyriaki.

As we approached the house we could see grandmother standing in the shade of the pomegranate tree at the entrance of her garden waiting for us. She was a stout woman with round shoulders. She was dressed in a simple, plain black blouse and long village skirt. On her head she wore a black *kouroukla*,* a light cotton kerchief that covered her hair. Her smiling face seemed weather worn but exuded an ambience of kindness. Grandmother welcomed us. She kissed mother and then she kissed my sister and me with her special warmth. She embraced and showered us with kindly kisses.

"Welcome, my daughter, welcome, my children," she said showing concern in her eyes.

"*The Panayia* *has helped you on your journey to me."

Her embrace felt hot and damp, her kiss left the perspiration of her face on my cheek. Inside, her house felt cool, it was a relief to be out of the scorching sun; she gave us water from the huge clay urn that stood in a dark corner of the kitchen.

"Come and drink some water to cool you down and to bring you to your senses after all the heat that you have endured on that awful bus."

The water that she proffered to us was brought daily from the village well and after our long journey it felt cold in our dry mouths and instantly refreshed us.

My mother and sister stayed for a day or two and then they had to return to Varosi. Mother tried to explain matters to me in a gentle manner.

"Mama and Kika are going to Varosi because I have to work and Kika has to go to school and there will be no one to look after you. You will have to stay with grandmother but mama and Kika will be back very soon to see you."

"Are you going to come tomorrow, mama?" I asked.

"No, it will not be as soon as that. I will be here to see you after two or three weeks. Don't worry, mama and Kika will not be very far away and grandmother will look after you."

I could not really understand what she was trying to say and only realised the meaning when she wrapped the few things that grandmother had prepared for her into a small bundle and then with my sister walked slowly to the bus stand at the centre of the village. The bus was already there and people were boarding. Mother looked at me and said,

"It's time for us to go, my darling, because mama needs to go to work and there is no one to look after you in Varosi."

I then understood that mother and Kika were going and that I would be left behind.

"I'm going with you to Varosi, I don't want to stay here! I'm going with you!" I shouted with indignation.

Grandmother took me firmly by the shoulders and held me. She spoke calmly but with a firm voice.

"You cannot go with mama this time, Fotaki. Your mama has to go to work and Kika will be at school, there is no one to look after you. You have to stay here in the village for a while. It will be alright, I promise you. I will tell you lots of stories. Now, calm down," she said in a strained voice.

I wriggled out of grandmother's grip and clutched at my mother as if I was a drowning swimmer trying to save myself. I would not let her go. I desperately held on tight to her, not wanting to be abandoned. I suffered the extreme fear of every little child of being deserted by his or her mother. I could not bear the thought of not going with her. I clutched onto her hand. I grabbed her feet as she boarded the bus. My grandmother now tightly embraced me and called out reassuringly,

"Get on the bus quickly, both of you and leave him to me. Don't worry. I will soon calm him down."

"Look after him properly, I will be back in two weeks," my mother tearfully replied. Meanwhile, I continued screaming while salty tears rolled down my hot cheeks.

"Mama!" I pleaded, "Don't leave me here, take me with you."

There was no consolation, there was no way out. The bus drove off leaving behind it a trail of dust carrying my mother and sister away while I remained disconsolate and inconsolable. After they had gone I refused to go back to the house until I was eventually enticed by grandmother's reassuring words.

For the rest of the day, I followed grandmother around the house, into the yard and back again while she continued reassuring me that mama would soon be back again.

"Mama is coming back very soon and she will bring you lots of sweets. If you are a good boy you will also have a very lovely toy."

I soon stopped crying and when it was time for bed, grandmother told me another of her magical stories about princes and princesses who had lived in far off lands long, long ago. Very soon, I was asleep at the end of what had been a difficult day.

*baranga - a small, simple dwelling for poor people, usually with a corrugated iron roof.

*Varosi - the modern town of Famagusta that was mostly inhabited by Greek Cypriots until they were forced to abandon it during the 1974 Turkish invasion. Varosi is today a "ghost town". Its Greek Cypriot citizens are prevented from returning to their homes by the Turkish Occupation forces. The Turkish Cypriots live in the old town of Famagusta inside the Venetian walls.

*Venetian walls – The walls of the city of Famagusta were originally built by the Lusignans. The Venetians later strengthened them and added further fortifications. In the 1571 Ottoman siege, the walls were neither breached nor captured. It was disease and starvation that forced the defenders to surrender.

*Stylloi village is on the old road from Famagusta to Nicosia that stretches across the Mesaoria plain. It was a mixed village of both Greek and Turkish Cypriots who enjoyed brotherly relationships until the ethnic violence of the late 1950s and early 1960s. The village was abandoned by its Greek Cypriot inhabitants during the Turkish invasion of 1974.

*Plythari - a type of brick made from mud mixed with straw then baked in the sun. This process caused the brick to harden so that it became durable even in wet weather. The houses built from plythari would be cool in the summer and retained heat during cold weather.

*Kouroukla - a light cotton or linen kerchief worn by women for modesty and for protection from the sun. A black kouroukla indicated that a woman had been widowed. The kouroukla is also worn in the Balkans by women of the Orthodox faith.

*The Panayia - The Virgin Mary, Mother of God. She is highly venerated by Greek Cypriots who often pray to her particularly during times of personal or national crises.

Grandmother

Grandmother's simple home was a hive of activity and a hubbub of noise. It was a traditional Cyprus house of the type that was most common in the villages before the 1950s. It was on one level in the shape of a rectangle divided into three parts. The middle section had the front and back entrances. This served as a sitting area and usually had a table and chairs. This is where guests were received and where the family sat during their time together. To the right was the kitchen where food was stored and meals prepared. To the left was the bedroom with an iron bed and the *armary*, a huge wardrobe with a strong lock so that the family valuables could be safely deposited. People, depending on their financial means, could add further rooms to the original design.

My aunties regularly visited the house bringing their children, my cousins, with them. There was often a flock of children who ran from the house into the yard and back. They talked and argued, they played and fought, they laughed and cried. There were no dull moments and there was no boredom. Neighbours and friends were always coming in and out.

Grandmother was the seamstress of the village measuring, cutting, fitting and making dresses. Her Singer sewing machine was driven by foot pedal. She busied herself making dresses, cleaning, cooking and looking after the children. And how she seemed to love it! Around her gathered her grand children like little chicks. She showered them with a warm ambience and adoration. But when grandfather used to come home in the evening all the noise ceased. Everything became hushed and subdued. The children stopped running around, the friends and neighbours sensed that it was time to go home. They quickly wished us goodnight and with their departure peace and quiet descended upon the house. The only sound that could be heard was the noise from grandmother's footsteps as she moved around the kitchen getting ready our evening meal. She prepared the supper which was usually fried potatoes mixed with eggs and onions. Sometimes she boiled beans with potatoes that were sprinkled with olive oil, lemon and salt. There was always lots of bread that grandmother baked once a week in the *fournos*, the earthen oven that was in her garden at the back of the house. The plates of food were put on *a paneri**that was placed on a stool. We ate in silence and in awe of our brooding grandfather.

Grandmother was a great story teller. She could tell stories in a marvellous and unforgettable manner. I looked forward to the story telling hour with great relish. Apart from playing out with the other village children, I liked nothing better then the stories that my grandmother told. She would lie in the middle of her high iron bed like some elderly Scheherazade,* with my sister Kika on one side and with me on the other. She always waited for us to ask. My sister with surprising confidence always asked first.

"Tell us a story, grandmother, please," she said.

"Yes, tell us a story," I pleaded.

She waited until everything was still and silent. From either side we looked up at her smiling, gentle face, feeling her warmth and absolute love. Then she began...

"Once upon a time, long ago, far over the mountains and across the seas..."

Her tone always expressed the magical or mysterious quality of the story; her telling of the story became rhythmic so that it had a momentum that evolved as it was spoken. It always gripped our attention. We felt the suspense in our hearts as the stories of handsome princes and beautiful princesses, witches and goblins, mermaids and of fantastic sea voyages to magical far off lands unfolded to inspire our childish imaginations.

Her story telling was a wonderful experience and my memory of that has never faded. Grandmother looked after my sister and me with her warmth and tenderness. She blessed us in her simple devout manner and prayed that we should become teachers or doctors for the benefit of mankind and who, in her estimation, were the most important people in society.

On the day when we were going to depart for England, she came to Varosi with grandfather, my aunts, my uncles and cousins to bid us farewell. The separation was for her a painful experience. She didn't quite understand the geography, the distances involved. For her it may have been like travelling to another town on the island. She begged my mother not to go for she feared that my father would continue to prove unreliable. She reminded my mother that he was a gambler and a drinker. Mother, however, remained determined that she should join her husband for better or for worse. For grandmother, it was obvious that mother was taking a very big risk because she was going to leave her relatives behind and in a new country she would not have the family support that she had hitherto enjoyed.

Grandmother was a simple village person who knew little about the world. I suppose if one was to say to her that the Earth was flat and that the moon was made from cheese she would not question it because such matters had never been made relevant to her through a process of normal, basic education. For her, the whole planet consisted of Cyprus and a few other well known countries. She was typical of many women of her generation in Cyprus who worked extremely hard, bore children but who were never given the opportunity to discover anything about the world. Grandmother's lack of education was balanced by the great love that she had for her family. Her simple understanding of the world and her great love is exemplified in the following story:

She had never heard of the town of Aberfan in Wales. Well, when mother, my sister and I had been in England for some time, a terrible tragedy struck the people of the small coalmining town of Aberfan. Aberfan was surrounded by coal slag heaps from the local mines. Tragically, heavy rain caused movement in the mounds; on the 21st October, 1966, there was a landslide that sent thousands of tonnes of coal slag on to the nearby houses and a junior school that stood in the way of the torrent. The time was just after 9.00am in the morning when it happened. It was a terrible accident in which 130 people died - mainly school children and their teachers who were buried alive.

The news of this very sad event travelled fast even to Stylloi in Cyprus where grandmother immediately began to mourn the death of my sister and me. She was a simple soul who loved much but who had very little understanding of the world beyond her village. She imagined that in England, where we had gone to, there was only one school just like in Stylloi and that my sister and I were amongst the children of the school who had lost their lives when the mud had submerged the school. She was reassured by those around her that Aberfan was far away from London where we lived but she was not convinced until a letter arrived from my mother and father informing her that we were not involved in the tragic accident that had befallen the unfortunate people of Aberfan. In the letter, father tried to explain that England was not a big village but that it was a big country that had many great cities, much greater and much bigger than even Nicosia and that it had thousands of towns and villages of which Aberfan was only one. It was as if he was trying to explain something to a little child who needed everything to be expressed in very simple terms. He did not mention that Aberfan is a place in Wales because he had no wish to confuse his distraught mother-in-law any further. By a gradual process grandmother was made to understand that my sister and I were safe and sound.

*Paneri - this was made from straw tightly woven together into the shape of a round board approximately the size of a small table top and when placed on a flat surface such as a stool; it could function as a small table top. It was often decorated in traditional folk patterns. After use it could be hung on the wall for ornamental purposes.

*Sheherazade is the heroine storyteller in the tales of "One Thousand and One Arabian Nights". The Sultan who has been disappointed in marriage is determined to avenge himself by taking a bride every day and then executing her the morning after the consummation. Sheherazade, however, on the night of her wedding, cleverly entertains the Sultan with a story that she does not complete by morning when she is due to be executed. The Sultan is so keen to hear the end of the story that he spares her life for that day. The next night Sheherazade repeats the same rouse until eventually the Sultan recognizes her special qualities, falls in love with her and they live, as the story goes, happily ever after.

Grandfather

I hardly ever saw grandmother and grandfather speaking together. Grandfather left home before sunrise and returned after dark. My grandmother served his food and he ate in silence and in silence we would all sit around watching him. He had down cast eyes and a long moustache with dropping ends. He was old even then but his sturdy frame filled the doorway. He was like some hero out of Homer's epics. His wife and daughters were respectful and obedient towards him. I now realise that perhaps they feared him somewhat, for he had a terrible temper. He was at least six feet in height; he had dark eyes and straight grey hair that lay flat over his forehead. He wore high boots and carried a *matsouka*, a heavy shepherd's staff. He was a master shepherd who herded sheep from dawn to dusk.

His dog was called Frixos who was always never far from him. Frixos had smooth black hair on his back and long yellow hair on his underbelly. He was a large, impressive dog, more like a wolf then a sheep dog . He was loveable towards familiar people but hostile towards strangers at whom he snarled until grandfather would call him to heal. He was a diligent and hard working dog, eager to please his owner. In the fields, master and dog worked like a team. Grandfather whistled instructions that sent the dog to harry the sheep to the right or to the left. Sometimes when a sheep strayed from the flock Frixos ran at it, he barked and growled; he blocked its path, turned it around then speedily chased it back to reunite with the flock. Grandfather loved his dog like a true friend.

One day, when grandfather had come home from tending the sheep, grandmother prepared the evening meal and put it on the *paneri*. Grandfather was exhausted from wandering in the fields with his sheep all day long under the hot sun. He washed his hands in a bowl of water then sat down to have his supper. No sooner had he sat down to eat when the cat that had been sleeping in the corner of the room smelt the food, sauntered lazily over to where we were sitting and hopped onto the *paneri*. As fast as lightening grandfather grabbed the cat and threw it hard upon the wall. He cursed and blasphemed like a madman. The cat screeched and ran out with its hair on end. His anger ceased and he sat down again quiet and composed while we continued to look on, not daring to utter a word to him. His cruel treatment of the cat was in contrast to his feelings for his dog.

Many years after, during a casual conversation, my sister revealed some family secrets relating to grandfather.

"Oh, didn't you know that grandfather's mother was Turkish?" she asked. "And her name was Fatima. * You see, it was a matter of the heart. His father was called George and he was a hired Shepherd for a rich Turkish Cypriot landowner in Trikomo. As it happened, George, our great grandfather somehow met with Fatima and they both fell in love with each other."

I listened with utter interest as my sister continued to reveal the love story.

"Well, love doesn't recognise religious or racial differences. Race and religion don't mean a thing when you are in love. The two conspired and ran away together. Despite the threats and counter threats from the families, Fatima was baptised and became Christina and she married our great grandfather George. It was a real 'Romeo and Juliet' story with a happy ending." She then added as an after thought, "Perhaps Cyprus might have been a much happier place if more people had followed their example."

This was a revelation to me. We had always been so proud of our Hellenic identity and suddenly we were not entirely what we thought we were. Now, we live in a time and place when we can accept mixed marriages but I can only have great sympathy for my great grandfather and great grandmother, who disregarded all conventions dividing the two communities of Cyprus for the sake of their love. They were like two heroic characters in some romantic novel or film who would not allow anything to prevent them from fulfilling their love. They must have had unbelievable courage and belief in each other to challenge the powerful and entrenched rules of their society.

This family story certainly prompted me to examine my feelings towards the 'so called' historic enemies of the Greek people. As a child I had been subjected to my fair share of anti Turkism through my exposure to the standard educational issues of reading books from the Greek Ministry of Education that were also available to Greek Cypriot children living in England. These books presented the Turks as a barbaric horde intent on destroying Greek Christian civilization. Another influence that had contaminated my view of Turks and presented them as thieves, rapists and cold blooded killers was the Greek press whose newspapers were widely available in the Cypriot cafes and shops in London. I am certain that the Turkish Ministry of Education and the Turkish press were doing an equally thorough job in teaching the Turkish people about how the Greek Army had invaded Anatolia in 1920 and committed heinous crimes against the Turkish Nation and that all Greek Cypriots wanted to murder the Turkish Cypriots and proclaim union with Greece.

The discovery that my great grand mother was a Turkish Cypriot should not have surprised me because it is pretty obvious that there has been intermingling between the two peoples in Cyprus despite the conventions that prevented Moslems and Christians from marrying. In fact, the pure race theory isn't credible and particularly so in Cyprus. Unfortunately, the Cypriots, like the Capulets and the Montaques, in Shakespeare's tragedy of feuding families in Verona, have not been perceptive enough to notice the many wonderful things which could unite them. Instead, they have emphasised their small differences and these have been used as an excuse for hate and division. Cyprus, like the Montaques and the Capulets, who suffer the loss of their children, remains on the verge of a similar tragedy. At least for our family there was in this instance a happy ending, the romance of our great grand parents resulted in a fruitful marriage with the birth of many descendents. There were many such stories in Cyprus which were hushed up with the gathering nationalistic storm that devastated the island from the about the mid 1950s.

~

As a child mother was a shepherdess, tending flocks of sheep with her father on the wide plain of Mesaoria that in spring time exploded into colour. Grey clouds would gather low over the land and the heavy rain turned the dry and dusty plain into a carpet of deep green grass, speckled with the yellow and white narcissus. The streams that had dried up during the summer months filled and flowed. Sometimes their banks burst, quenching the thirst of the dry soil that for a few weeks became a rich tapestry of flowers, as if woven in fine silk. Oregano and thyme grew in rich abundance, exuding powerful aromas of earth and spice. Mesaoria was a place full of hard working country people tending their flocks in the busy season of lambing or where sunburnt men expertly guided their horse drawn ploughs, clicking at the horses, cutting long straight farrows into the rich soil, preparing their fields for the sowing of seed while inwardly praying for the success of the crop so that children, wives and elderly parents would not hunger during the coming winter.

Like the blossom of the lemon tree, the spring does not endure for very long in Cyprus. The heat of summer rushes in with vengeful, burning intensity.

In Mesaoria, my mother spent her childhood years with her father, helping to tend flocks of sheep. From dawn to dusk, winter or summer, they trekked across the plain grazing their sheep. Mother knew, however, that many other children of the village went to school and she sometimes summoned the courage to ask,

"Father, when shall I go to school?"

The older she became the more often she asked this question and grandfather avoided giving her an answer. He would move on as if to tend the sheep, whistling commands to Frixos, his dog, and calling out to the sheep.

On one rare occasion grandfather looked at his little daughter and attempted to answer the question that she constantly asked. He did not often engage in conversation with others nor was he a man who showed any eagerness to express his ideas. He always preferred to keep his thoughts to himself as if he was reluctant to trust those around him or perhaps he remained silent because he could not give a pleasing answer to his questioner. On this occasion, his little daughter's direct and courageous challenge made him feel that he was obliged to at least try to explain something about the injustice of life that made it difficult for a little girl, who wanted to learn how to read and write, to attend school.

"Andriani," he began his answer to the question slowly and deliberately, pausing to think carefully about his choice of words.

"Andriani, you know that I was never sent to school by my father and to this day I do not know how to read and write and neither did my father before me. I know that not being able to read and write is like being blind because we cannot understand much of what is in God's creation."

"But in school I can learn, father. I can begin to become something more than a person who doesn't know anything about the world. I know that school will help me to become something wonderful in this life. My god sisters are going to school and they are already reading. I sometimes go to their house and they allow me to sit with them while they are reading from their books. It is a wonderful thing to learn letters, to read and to write. Why am I here in the fields looking after sheep from morning until dusk? Why am I not at school with the other children? What will I ever learn looking after sheep day after day?"

"Do you think, Andriani, that I have the means to send you to school but for some selfish reason I refuse? No, you are quite mistaken. Kanikli, your godfather, is the richest man in the village. He has more land and more herds of animals than any other man in this area. He has the money to send your god sisters to school. In comparison to him, we have very little. He has money, that is why his daughters go to school and we are poor, that is why your help is needed for the sustenance of our family. That is why you are not at school."

He abruptly stopped speaking; he looked down at the earth as if in troubled thought then looked again at his little daughter who continued to have an apprehensive and troubled expression on her face.

"Who knows?" he said, "only Almighty God knows the future. One day, perhaps, you will go to school."

He gave her a rare and encouraging smile and then they continued their walk across the fields, saying very little, leading their sheep on to fresh pastures.

~

I know that school was important to mother because as an adult she often spoke about it. During the 1920s there was a great deal of poverty in Cyprus and it seemed more useful for a child, particularly for a girl to help her parents with work in the fields, gathering in the harvest or looking after the sheep of a rich landowner to earn a few rials for the needs of the family. It seemed however, that my mother's question about going to school weighed heavily on the mind of her father. He had struck a bargain with the village school teacher for my mother to attend school and in return my mother would clean the teacher's house. She would earn a few rials and with this money she would buy the books that she needed for her lessons.

My mother was delighted and was able to briefly attend the village school for a very short period of time. Not being able to carry on must have been a great disappointment to her but her help was needed to earn a little more money for the support of the family.

~

Though education was entirely free in England, it was not so in Cyprus that had been annexed by the British in 1914 and had formally become a crown colony in 1925. In Cyprus, poor families had to buy their books for primary school and secondary education was beyond the reach of the vast majority of Cypriots. So, without books it was difficult for my mother to continue with even the basics of reading and writing. In this day and age, it seems awful that a child should be desperate to learn, should hunger for an education and to be deprived of the opportunity because of the lack of a few pennies that would pay for books. Mother was deprived but she always retained her desire to learn. I can clearly remember how, as an adult, she cared for her family, worked from morning until night and at the same time struggled to teach herself reading and writing. She often, with great concentration, tried to decipher a text, reading and rereading each word slowly and carefully. She began to read individual words and then sentences and whole pages and eventually she read whole books. She showed the capacity to learn and often said to us with a smile on her face and a voice full of emotion,

"If I had had the opportunities that you young people have today, I would have become something marvellous."

Looking back, I think that it was no idle boast; she would certainly have achieved something stunning.

Her parents named her Andriani and it was a name entirely suitable for her because it means manly strength. I know that her life experiences often required an enormous amount of spiritual and psychological endurance for her to survive. A real test of her strength was her marriage because, though father was a kind and loving man, he was also often irresponsible. It seems that when she married him, his family felt that mother was not an appropriate match. They considered themselves a rich family of landowners from Sotira while she was only a daughter of a shepherd from Stylloi. Looking back on their lives together, his marriage to mother was probably the best thing that he ever did! But his family did not realise it at the time.

When my parents married in 1942, they lived in Sotira for some time and this is where my sister Kika was born in November, 1943. Father had a shoe maker's shop. He was a master craftsman, able to measure, cut and hand stitch shoes and boots of every description. He often told the story with a sparkle in his eye about how he cycled to Paralimni from Sotira to learn his trade from a maestro who was reluctant to teach him.

"I would go to the work shop day after day," my father would say, "and this mean person made me spend hours on dyeing the leather instead of showing me the techniques of cutting and stitching. I had worked at the shop for a whole year before I was allowed to measure a customer for shoes. He did not want me to learn, he was afraid that I should become better then him and take his customers. So, do you know what I did?"

He would pause and smile at his own cunning.

"Whenever the maestro was working on a special pair of shoes that needed some delicate technique, I pretended to be busy somewhere close to him so that I could observe his methods. It wasn't the best way to learn but he forced me to become a thief of his craft because he did not want to teach me anything. I served a seven year apprenticeship and I learnt more than he was willingly to teach me."

The end of his story was always followed by a hearty laughter. In a more serious tone he always added an epilogue to his tale.

"In those days I was one of the more promising young men in the village. I was a master of a trade. I owned a fine bicycle made in Sheffield and I my family were wealthy and well established. My mother, your grandmother, had already spoken to me, my brother and my sister about our inheritance. I could look ahead to making a good life for myself... but then things went terribly wrong."

At this serious point in the story he smiled gently and changed the subject. Mother filled the gaps in information. Their time in the village was far from the idyllic life. Father was bad tempered, often cursing and shouting and at this time he became involved in a criminal adventure to rob the British Military Base of Acrotiri; the plan was to steal some barrels of oil. Father jokingly said that this was resistance against the British. The plan failed and father was even wounded as the gang tried to escape. As a child, I often noticed the scar of the flesh wound on his right shoulder.

It was prison for him and his accomplices. When he returned after the war, mother's life with him did not improve because prison seemed to have made him a less caring person. He sold what he had and wasted the money. They were left penniless. Even after many years, mother would still become distressed speaking about this period in her life. Her distress was so great that while pregnant she felt such anguish that she aborted her pregnancy. She saw no future and no hope. She did not know how she would be able to look after my sister because another baby would have meant that she would have been unable to work and she certainly could not rely on father.

My sister and I were the only two people that mother ever spoke to about this period in her life and she did this when we were mature adults. She only spoke of those sad events if the subject of the conversation happened to stray onto how difficult life was during the war years and their aftermath. She always seemed a happy and optimistic individual but when speaking about the events of this time her countenance changed; her eyes filled with sorrow and her face suddenly aged beyond its years.

"This was the blackest period of my life," she began and as she spoke the room that we were in became sombre and still as if in sympathetic sadness at her painful memories.

"I knew that he was sometimes foolish but I imagined that after giving birth to you, Kika, your father would have become more settled and more responsible. He did not and like a fool he went from one crisis to another, dragging us along with him."

There was a hint of anger in her voice even though the events that she was describing had happened long ago.

"It was a terrible time for me because after he came out of prison he seemed much worse than before. He didn't care about the consequences of his actions. It was at this time that I became pregnant again and for me it was a sign of hope. I thought that perhaps with our second child he would show more concern and understanding for us. His mother had given him and his brother a plot of land each next to her own house so that they could build homes for their families. The building materials were all bought and ready. In spring the builders were due to begin the work. It was not to be. I was making plans for our future but unfortunately, your father had other ideas. In one mad, catastrophic week he changed our lives forever. He sold the building materials meant for constructing our house; he took the money and went to Nicosia where he indulged himself in his vices. Then he returned and did not tolerate one word to be spoken about this matter. Over night we had become without the prospect of being able to build our own home and we were penniless. I withdrew into a silent trauma not believing the utter madness of what he had done and when in my despair I looked at my growing womb I walked out of the house into the dark night, I picked two heavy rocks from the ground and ....."

She always paused at this point in the story, unable to continue, as if her heart would burst. Tears filled her dark eyes as she visually recalled this dreadful episode in her life.

"I felt that this world was very harsh and I did not want to bring another child into all this suffering."

My sister and I never questioned mother further about the dreadful events. We understood that every now and then she needed to repeat this story because despite the passing of the years, the wounds had not healed nor would they ever. The retelling must have provided some momentary catharsis, a relief to the troubled soul. When she finished speaking she wiped the tears from her face, sighed deeply and made an effort to cheer up.

"At least I have both of you my children, close to me. May God forgive me for the wrong things that I have committed in my moments of weakness," she said, trying to smile so that her sadness would not also affect us, her listeners.

Yet, like many other women in Cyprus during the 1950s, she saw no other life beyond that she had with her husband. It seems that for most women during this period there was no escape from the marriage bond, even in relationships that were for them very destructive.

Indeed, it would be many years before Cypriot women would be able to gain control over their own destinies

The family then moved from Sotira to Stylloi where they continued to live in dire poverty and where I was born in April, 1950. I suppose mother moved there to be nearer her own family who at least might give her some support. Her mother and father would be at hand as well as her younger sister Eleni who was as yet unmarried. They looked after us so that mother could seek work either in the village, labouring in the fields or perhaps find work in Varosi. Regular work was very hard to come by, particularly in the village and travelling to Varosi from Stylloi was difficult on a daily basis. Before long father had began to talk about moving yet again, this time to live in Varosi where work could be found on a more regular basis.

---

*It is probable that Fatima was not ethnically Turkish. Her family may have been Greek Orthodox Christians who had converted to Islam. These people were called "Linobambaki" which is translated as linen/cotton. It indicated that such people were neither Greek nor Turkish. Neither were they entirely Christian nor Moslem, neither, the one or the other, but they were something in between. Christian Greeks sometimes converted to Islam so that they could be granted rights that were only enjoyed by the ruling Moslems. Eventually, the Linobambaki blended entirely into the Turkish Cypriot community.

To Varosi

Though there was much poverty in Cyprus during the immediate aftermath of the Second World War, there was also a sense of things beginning to get back on track. There were service families from Britain and mother found work with them, cleaning their houses. She worked so hard for a few pennies; for the poor it was always just for a few pennies. She cleaned two or three of their houses every day.

We had moved to Varosi by then and lived in a *baranga*, a short distance from the beach that would one day be developed into a tourist resort with luxury hotels and in turn be abandoned with the onslaught of the Turkish invasion of 1974.

The *baranga* was a kind of cabin, a rectangular one room structure made from wood, corrugated iron and some bricks. I remember that our *baranga* had marble floor tiles that were broken and they had space in between the cracks so that you could see the dark earth beneath. From our *baranga* mother set off each morning at sunrise marching off to work like a courageous soldier. At the end of the day my sister and I often stood at the door of our *baranga* peering into the night waiting for our mother to emerge from the darkness.

"When is mama coming home, is she coming soon?" I asked my sister over and over again, fearing that I wouldn't see her again. My sister comforted me,

"Don't worry, Fotaki, mama will soon be home, I promise you."

Eventually mother returned weary after the day's battle, long after the sun had gone down.

There was no negotiation regarding how hard she had to work because if you did not work you would not eat. Nobody was going to help you or give some kind of assistance. Mother understood that there were no benefits to be had from anywhere. Most people lived from hand to mouth and it was only the sense of family that prevented the very poor from becoming destitute and homeless. Elderly parents would take in their grown up children and their families, brothers and sisters shared what they had with each other. "Blood is thicker then water," some people often said in acknowledgement of the bonds that enabled them to survive in difficult times. Like countless other poor, working people, mother needed money to put food on the table and counted herself very fortunate that she had now a job to go to and daily thanked God in her prayers that she had been blessed with the vigorous health and strength to work for the benefit of her children.

When I wasn't being looked after by my grandparents, my sister had to stay at home to care for me at the cost of her education. Even years after my mother's childhood, children were still kept away from school to help maintain the family. The choices were difficult but had to be made.

I was then, about 4 or 5 years of age. It is the time that we begin to have a memory of our lives and I can remember that time with some clarity.

Close to our baranga, across some parched fields and a main road along which hardly any traffic could be seen was the beach of Varosi. The fine, golden sand stretched from the rocky outcrop below the Constantia Restaurant for two miles along the margin of the bay to Nea Salamina, founded by the heroes of Troy and which had once been the rich capital of King Evagoras who fought the Persian Empire for the liberty of Cyprus. On this dazzling beach, before the coming of tourism, the local children gathered to play.

I loved that time. I ran around all day long under the hot sun, dressed in only a pair of shorts, playing to my heart's content, not realising how nervous mother was that being a child and unaware of danger I could be swept out to sea if the weather suddenly changed.

She often told my sister who was only about 12 years of age to look out for me and never let me out of her sight. My poor sister, being frightened of the consequences threateningly articulated by mother, never let me out of her sight. She followed me everywhere and I made her life more difficult by refusing to ever go home before mother was due to arrive and this was often after nightfall.

Despite mother's long hours at work, we sometimes had no food to eat and felt the pangs of hunger; even so, we were not unhappy because we could play all day long without having an adult standing over us. We tolerated and endured our hunger because we had that freedom which all children desire and value. We could roam around, play, laugh, argue, fight and then make up again. We played to our hearts content and without adults to restrict us in any way. We could play at our favourite haunt, the Varosi beach with its golden sand and clear blue waters. In the summer, the fine sand became so hot that the unaccustomed found it too hot to tread on but it didn't burn us for we had developed resistance to the heat so that we could walk or run around without any discomfort. The lack of adult supervision had led me to feel that I could take chances but this was a mistake that my mother very soon made me regret.

One day, on the feast day of the Hrisosotiros ,The Golden Saviour, when the *paniyiri* * was held in the village of Sotira, mother planned to take us there for the day. It was still early in the morning and there were things that she needed to do. Our Aunt Eleni, mother's younger sister, was with us.

"Mama, I want to play on the beach. Why can't I play on the beach? I want to go to the beach. My friends are at the beach. Why can't I go?"

I kept repeating this to wear her will down so that she would give in to my demand.

"No, because very soon we are going to the *paniyiri*," she answered patiently.

"No, mama, I want to go to the beach!"

She soon relented to my constant demands. Perhaps she might have been very tired from work because it was out of character for her to relent to my wishes. She had always tried and continued in the years ahead of us to maintain a firm discipline on my sister and me so that no harm might befall us. But on this occasion she relented:

"Don't go to the rocks at the Constantia, there are deep pools. If you fall in you will drown. Stay opposite the path from our baranga. Do you promise me not to go near the rocks?" she uttered, giving me an anxious, parental look.

I nodded vigorously to affirm that I understood but all I wanted to do was to get away as quickly as possible. I knew that I had got my way and I was delighted to resume my usual play.

I had a stick in my hand and having been told not to do something had the opposite effect on me: I headed straight to the far left of the beach where the rocks protruded like jagged, uneven teeth, half hidden by the sand and water.

In the centre of this out crop there were deep pools of a clear blue ocean decorated with white coral rock and green, sea plants through which dozens of little multicoloured fish roamed in and out. This was my favourite place on the beach and where, though forbidden to me, I often came to play solitary games in which I lost myself in some imaginary world while precariously balancing on the edge of a rock over looking a deep watery cavern.

Disobediently, I made my way to the edge of the pool that was surrounded by sharp coral. The pool was clear, clean and deep. There was nobody else around. Had I fallen in I would have surely drowned.

I launched my stick into the pool and imagined that it was the ship of Odysseus. I'd recently heard the story of Odysseus and the Cyclops at school and I had been thrilled by it. I was lost in the child's world of play and imagination, creating my own imaginary characters and adventures as I moved dangerously from rock to rock that overlooked the deep pool. I was immersed in Homer's world of storms and shipwrecks, escaping from cannibalistic giants and witches that turned men into beasts. Odysseus was my captain and we were having a great time. Suddenly there was an unexpected interruption. I was awoken from my day dream by a calm, quiet voice:

"Fotaki..."

It was mother. At the sound of her voice Odysseus and his crew, one eyed Polyphemos and his tribe of one eyed Cyclopes quickly disappeared back into the depths of my childish imagination. My captain had abandoned me as Homer's world disappeared and I was back at the rocky pool with mother standing a few feet away from me, trying not to show her anger.

"Fotaki, slowly, my child! Don't be frightened!"

I looked at her and felt her tension. I reached out to get my stick from the pool.

"Oh, be careful! Don't fall in!"

I'd managed to retrieve my stick. Then she said more quietly,

"Now, come closer towards me."

I remember that she had a very quiet voice and continued to smile strangely at me. I still felt frightened when I looked at her. Instinctively, I knew something wasn't right. And on that hot, mid morning when she'd grabbed hold of my hand and dragged me onto the safety of the sand away from the dangerous rocks, her scream at me expressed the fears and frustrations of her stressful life. She hit me across the legs with my small stick. I cried and struggled while she dragged me home, my hand tightly clutched in a firm grip with no possibility of escape.

When we got home, her sister Eleni was very upset to see that I had been punished so severely. I was then washed and dressed in my best clothes and I'd soon stopped crying. My mother then hugged me and in tears, feeling guilty, she tried to justify the punishment that she had inflicted upon me.

"Rather than me crying for him, let him cry for his disobedience and naughtiness!"

The punishment had the desired effect. I would never again stray towards the dangerous rocks.Later, my sister used this prohibition as a means of controlling me. She often warned me,

"If you don't listen, I shall tell mama that you went to the rocks again."

At the thought of being so severely punished again, I reluctantly obeyed my sister who was delighted that she could at last exert some kind of control over me. The rocks also became a kind of symbol between my mother and me so that as a child or even later in life when I became a man, if she felt that I was making an erroneous decision she would quietly utter,

" Fotaki, be careful , you are too close to the rocks."

Of course, I understood her implied meaning .

---

*Paniyiri – a village fare that takes place on the holy day of the patron saint of the village. The village people attend church on such a day when special prayers are dedicated to the patron saint of the village. This is followed with a celebration in the centre of the village. There is food and drink, music and song. Stalls are set up that sell cakes, sweets, nuts, toys. It is a family occasion when people gather together to enjoy each others company.

Paniyiri

In the afternoon we travelled to the paniyiri in Sotira. We travelled the short journey from Varosi on a crowded bus full of people heading for the celebration of the feast day.

On our arrival, we found that the crowds had already gathered. There were many stalls selling sweets and cakes. Long sticks of delicious *sougouko** were laid out on display. Trays of *galatoboureko,* khataiffi** and *kalo pragma** tempted all those who walked by and looked upon them. There was cooling *mahalebi** eaten with a sprinkling of sugar and rose water. There was the smell of *souvlakia** everywhere. People were sitting in the cafes eating and drinking. Families in their best clothes were strolling through the festive streets. Girls in bright floral dresses walked hand in hand, boys in clean, crisp white shirts loitered in groups of two or three trying to catch the attention of the girls who walked by and teasingly looked at the boys, children called out to each other and ran around playing their games. There was the sound of music and laughter as people greeted each other and stopped to speak in the village centre. This was the day of Hrisosotiros, the Golden Saviour, after whom the village was named. This was the day when men and women put their troubles behind them, at least for a few hours, for the purpose of worship and then for relaxation.

Here, my aunties and uncles with their children came to greet us. Mother was always delighted to be amongst her sisters. Each one had her own pronounced character: Eleni was the youngest and the loveliest. She darted around arranging things, keeping an eye on the children and making sure that everything went smoothly. Christina was the most reserved. She spoke quietly and in moderate tones avoiding gossip and loud people. Filou always had a smile for every one and she was famous for her ability in the *tsatista* *songs. On the first occasion when I visited Cyprus as an adult and with my family, Auntie Filou invited us to her house for dinner. Not only was the food and wine delicious but Auntie Filou also composed and sang many *tsatista* songs to welcome us to Cyprus. Auntie Martha was the most out spoken. She was very courageous and challenged anything that might be an injustice. Of all my aunties she had a special warmth and kindness towards other people. Mother and her sisters were known as the five sisters from Stylloi who had come to Sotira and claimed *Sotirkates* , men of Sotira, for husbands.

When the sisters were together, they always created a sense of enjoyment. They would forget the problems of life. They laughed, joked and they talked, sharing their news and plans with each other. The *Paniyiri of the Hrisosotiros* was the time when they walked out with their husbands and their children , with pride and dignity, to enjoy the society of the village and to interact with friends and relatives.

The festivities continued into the late hours. Wine and KEO 31 Cyprus Brandy were consumed in great quantities especially by the men who competed with each other in the singing of *tsatista* to the accompaniment of the violin.

Eventually, the gratified villagers would begin to drift away from the village centre. They had eaten their fill of *souvlakia* and *kleftiko*. They had erased the after taste of pork and lamb with sweet meats. They had quenched their thirst with wine and brandy. On that night we were going to stay at Auntie Filous' house. Feeling tired but satisfied with the prolonged festivities, we walked through the streets with the scent of jasmine hanging heavily in the air, under a glowing, white moon and a sky dotted with stars lighting our way through the village streets.

* sougouko, galatoboureko, kalo pragma, mahalebi- sweetmeats.

* souvlakia- smallpieces of pork or lamb grilled on charcoal and wrapped in pitta bread.

*tsatista- songs composed on the spur of the moment in rhyming couplets to suit a particular occasion.

Aunt Cornelia

In the morning of the following day, mother took my sister and me to the village centre to buy us shoes because they were cheaper in the village then in Varosi. On the way it chanced that we encountered my father's sister, Aunt Cornelia, carrying some bags of shopping, on her way home. She was a small woman with a cheerful face. She greeted us with a warm smile,

"Kalimera sas."

She kissed my sister and me affectionately. She embraced mother like a long lost sister. Mother was rather surprised because father's family had been against his marriage with mother.

"You must come to the house, Andriana. My mother wants to see you and her grandchildren."

Something had obviously changed because their disapproval had now changed into a fond embrace. She wouldn't take no for an answer and mother soon relented. The house was only five minutes away and we were soon there.

"Come in, please come in," said my Aunt Cornelia, her sun burnt face beaming with an affectionate smile.

"Mother, where are you?" She called out towards the kitchen.

"Andrikou and the children are here."

Grandmother Margarita emerged from the kitchen wiping the perspiration from her face with her apron. Like all the old ladies of the village who were widowed, she was dressed in the customary black.

Her hair was tied back and covered with a *kouroukla*. She was stout and sturdy with strong hands that had laboured on the land. Her intelligent eyes were deep set and sparkled with warmth and intelligence.

"Kalosorisete , welcome my children. Why are you standing at the door like strangers, come in and sit down."

We were there almost for the whole morning. They offered us sweets and drinks that refreshed us. Grandmother asked many questions about where we lived in Varosi, whether mother had work and could support us. She also knew that father was working for the British in the Suez Canal and asked whether he kept in contact with us. Mother didn't want to upset the old lady by telling her the truth that father rarely sent us a letter or anything else.

"Yes, mother, Loizos sends us letters and money. We receive something every month from him. Don't worry about us. I have a job and everything is fine."

Grandmother Margarita was not convinced.

"I am not so sure that everything is alright as you say. I know that Loizos can be very foolish at times. I don't know why he sold the materials I had purchased for him to build his house. Why did he do such a thing and now you and your children do not have a place to call your own? You are like birds without a nest."

Her face was now full of tears at the thought of what her son had done and the implications for his family. Mother took her hand and tried to reassure her that despite everything that had happened, things would turn out for the best.

"Mother, Loizos is sorry for what he has done. He is now going to be more responsible. We are both young and strong. We will work hard and build a new future. Don't think about what has happened. It is the past."

" May God hear your words and help my son to become a better man for the sake of this children."

Grandmother Margarita spoke with feeling and conviction. She was pleased with mother's brave little speech but she didn't believe it for a moment because she knew her son too well. She now looked at mother with respect and admiration, clearly recognising that her son was very fortunate to be married to such a worthwhile person.

Their modern, brick built house stood on the site where the old family house had been for generations. The location was almost in the centre of the village, very close to the Church of the Hrisosotiros. The dwellings closest in proximity to the church belonged to the oldest and most established members of the village whose importance was also measured in the ownership of the rich and fertile land, cultivated fields that produced an abundance of Kolokassi* and potatoes as well as water melons, and a variety of vegetables that were sold at the municipal market of Varosi and which made the farmers of the area amongst the wealthiest in Cyprus.

Later, after our visit we laughed at how Aunt Cornelia had three or four children who each had one hand tied to the window frame by a kind of leash. She explained,

"There are passing cars and I don't want them to run out into the road, just in case."

Aunt Cornelia seemed happy enough when we visited her on that memorable occasion but she had gone through some problems which she would not have been able to sort out if it had not been for my father's actions. It might have been true that father had sometimes behaved in an irresponsible manner but sometimes he could also be very protective of the people whom he loved and cared for. Mother knew the story very well and often in an animated voice, as if the events had only happened yesterday, she would cast the plot in a manner that presented father as a hero and his brother- in- law as a villain. The truth of the matter is that she may have expressed some bias in her version of events. We listened to her in silence while mother thoroughly enjoyed the telling of the story:

"Old Kaiki was a very clever man in the village and he was also very fair. He had involved himself in civic matters and the villagers were so impressed by him that he became mayor, the *muchtari* of the village. His sons were good, hardworking boys and like their father were very ambitious. One of them, Panayi, saw the opportunity to gain more land and property through marrying a woman who could provide him with such wealth and in the village", mother continued, " it was a well known fact that Margarita, Cornelia's mother, at the death of her husband Pieris, had become the mistress of many plots of land around the village and beyond. Some of these were located as far as Macronissos, Ayia Thekli and even Ayia Napa. Cornelia was not a great beauty, but she was wealthy and for Panayi this seemed the most important consideration. In due course they were engaged and dear Cornelia soon fell pregnant. It is then that Panayi, began to show his true intentions. He wanted to get as much land as possible for marrying Cornelia and he was prepared to use blackmail."

At this point in the story, my mother would pause, smile and wait for a few seconds as if to create some kind of suspense in whoever was listening and even though I had heard this story a few times, the pause always worked well; I felt impatient for mother to resume from where she had left off:

"He began to show a great reluctance concerning his proposed marriage to Cornelia and complained that her dowry, and by this he meant the amount of land that on her wedding would be given as her share, was not enough. He threatened that he would not go through with the wedding unless this dowry was substantially increased. You can imagine how poor Cornelia felt. She was carrying a child; her fiancé was threatening to abandon her unless the family gave him more land. He had no shame and his greed prevented him from seeing the distress that he was causing to his pregnant fiancée and her mother. They didn't know what to do, they were at their wits end. And you must remember," mother added, "unmarried mothers in Cyprus at that time were looked down upon as a disgrace and in that village to have a child and no husband was a huge dishonour for the family. There would be no sympathy or understanding from anyone. Well, this is when Loizos, my husband took things into his own hands. When he heard what was happening from his mother, he obtained a pistol from God knows where and he let it be known that he was going to deal with Panayi if he dared to break his promise to marry his sister. Loizos took up position on a rooftop, apparently with serious intent. Very soon after, Panayi withdrew his threat to abandon his fiancée, and the wedding went ahead as planned. But this was not the end of the story. From the moment that my husband had interfered in this matter, Panayi developed an utter hatred for him. He and his brothers refused to allow him to attend the wedding of his sister and there was a probability that from that time onwards he tried very hard to claim even my husband's share of the inheritance."

My mother finished the telling of this story with an expression of anger and defiance on her face because she felt that we had been cheated by Panayi of what rightfully belonged to my father. Years after, when as a retired pensioner she returned to Sotira, she made her feelings clear that not only the plots of land that were my father's share of the inheritance had somehow ended up belonging to Panayi, but even the land upon which the house that Panayi inherited through marriage was a part of my father's share and had been stolen by him. Mother's claims were taken so seriously that Panayi's sons began to threaten this elderly woman who had returned to her husband's village after many years of living in a foreign land. Nothing came from the claims that mother had made simply because she didn't have any documents to prove ownership. When the matter was investigated at the local land registry, mother's feeling was that while the Kaiki family had been influential in the local government and the administration of village affairs, the documents and deeds showing my father's entitlement had been altered in favour of his sister and her husband Panayi. Of course, it may be that our grandmother Margarita and Aunt Cornelia had a hand in this because once the wedding had taken place and Panayi proved himself to be a good husband to Cornelia, they might have felt that it was only sensible to protect as much as possible of the family wealth and to prevent father from getting his hands onto it. Had he done so, it may have all been squandered in the gambling houses or the cabarets of Nicosia.

Despite the support he had given his sister during the crisis of her engagement, father's family had begun to think more realistically about him. They were already beginning to feel uncomfortable with his attitude and they saw very clearly that mother was a very decent and hardworking woman. They saw that she loved her children and cared for her husband, but he, on the other hand, was not to be trusted with property or money.

Many years after, I was to return to the family house in Sotira. I was welcomed by its sole occupant, Panayi, the widowed husband of my Aunt Cornelia. Even as an eighty year old he seemed sharp, alert and very aware of what was going on around him. When we met I called him uncle and tried to show my respect towards him to ally any fears that he may have had that I had returned and like my mother, to start making claims on the house in which he had lived for over fifty years. Even so, though he smiled graciously, he could not hide, I felt, his suspicion that I had returned to cause him some problems. He smiled and spoke politely but he glanced at me uneasily and had a strained expression on his face. Because I knew the details of the story I understood why Panayi may have been suspicious about my visit to Sotira.

Panayi's neighbour had been my father's brother, Uncle George who had been born and had always remained in the same house and had only left the village for very brief periods to journey to the near by towns on some essential business or other. Uncle George was a stout bald man with a rim of grey hair that stretched like a ribbon around the base of his head to just above his ears. His large, khaki brown eyes and bald head gave him the appearance of an ancient Greek philosopher. His crisp and witty speech added to the impression that he was an intelligent man. During my visit, I ventured to ask my uncle his views about my mother's claims. Uncle George had explained that the plot of land, upon which the house that Aunt

Cornelia occupied, was my father's but he had sold it to her and Panayi.

"Fotaki", my uncle addressed me in a formal manner befitting the serious subject of land ownership.

"Your father was never one to hold on to money for very long. He did not want the difficult life of a farmer. From the very beginning he did not want to stay here in this village. He sold the plot to our sister and enjoyed himself in the capital."

Uncle George was very direct and to the point regarding this matter. Mother claimed that he was not to be trusted and that he was in league with Panayi to cheat his own brother. She claimed that the plot for father's house belonged to him by right of inheritance but the Kaiki family had had the documents falsified in favour of Cornelia and thus under the control of Panayi, her husband. The truth of the matter is unclear and I have often asked the question to my sister that if father had not sold the plot for his house why had he never said that we had a right to it. He remained very quiet on the subject.

Near to the house that should have been my father's, was the old cemetery inside the compound of the church where generations of our family had been laid to rest. Here were our roots, our place of belonging. It seems that when father had lost his inheritance and particularly the plot of land, upon which his matrimonial home was intended to be built, he also thoughtlessly and selfishly tore out the roots that we, his family, could have had with the place where our forefathers had lived for generations. What he did then, without a doubt was the first step towards us becoming immigrants. First was the move from Sotira, where father had been a member of an established family, to Stylloi, where we lived in a house that was rented. There was no work available in this village and eventually it was decided to move to Varosi and from there, again for the same reasons, we embarked for England. We became a family without roots in its native soil, people who no longer had a precise geographical location, exiles of a sort, who like the wandering Jews of yester year would never again belong to a locality in the same sense as our grandparents had belonged to their communities.

It was much later, in a different environment that I gradually began to have a sense that when plants are torn from their native soil, some, the very old or the very established, suffer and die because they cannot again develop new roots in an alien soil. But there are also seedlings or young plants that acclimatise, take root in the new soil, nourish on its richness, establish themselves, grow, blossom and eventually bear fruit. Such would be our experience as we looked beyond the shores of our Mediterranean homeland, towards the northern climes, towards England.

*Kolokassi- a type of potato that is widely cultivated in Sotira and the surrounding villages.

A Bloody History

~

The 1950s were a difficult time for the Cypriot people. Even though the Second World War had ended in 1945 and a new, more prosperous Europe was beginning to emerge from the dust and devastation of war, civil war raged on in Greece for another five years bringing further misery to the Greek people.

At the beginning of the 1950s Cyprus remained a British Crown Colony. There had been attempts in the past to unite the island with Greece but these attempts were unsuccessful and only resulted in the bloody suppression of the people.

When the Greek War of Independence broke out in 1821, to pre-empt any difficulties with the populace of Cyprus, the Sultan authorised the execution of the leading members of Cypriot society. On the 9th of July of that tumultuous year, 486 prominent Christians including the Ethnarch, Archbishop Kyprianos, having been severely and cruelly tortured by the Ottoman authorities, were marched in the scorching midday sun, wounded, bleeding and bound in chains. They were marched to Sarai Square of Nicosia. I can imagine how the citizens of the capital must have had a sleepless and fearful night before the dawn of the day of the execution of their leaders. Families must have sat huddled together through the long night in fear of attack or even of massacre from the heavily armed Moslems who would stop at nothing in order to retain their control of the island.

Later that day, under the gaze of the terrified citizens of the capital, the Archbishop and the leaders of the church were offered their lives in return for denouncing the Christian faith and becoming followers of Islam. I can imagine how the proud and triumphant Kuchuk Pasha, the leader of the Turks, must have called out so that all could hear his offer:

"Those of you who will turn away from the cross and worship Allah the Almighty and Merciful, kiss the Koran, bow to Mohammed the Prophet and live as Moslems amongst us, will be spared from execution!"

The Bishops of the church with their Archbishop knelt together for the last time and prayed to Christ for the forgiveness of their sins and for the redemption of their souls. After their prayers, they walked in quiet dignity to their executions. Some prisoners were decapitated while others and amongst these the Ethnarch, were hanged on the branch of a mulberry tree. Not one of them had renounced his faith for the sake of his life. The blood from those who were beheaded flowed in streams and gathered in pools. One by one, while they called out to the Panayia or to Christ, their heads were cut off with a heavy sword, the *palla;* their heads were stacked into a pile that formed a pyramid. Heavily armed gangs of irregular Moslem militia continued to mercilessly beat those still awaiting execution. They screamed at the prisoners and at the stunned on lookers,

"Where is your Christos to save you? Where is your *Panayia* now? Embrace Almighty and Merciful Allah so that your worthless lives can be spared!"

The prisoners were prepared to die but they were not prepared to betray Christ or the *Panayia*. As if to inflict further pain on those who had been tortured and killed, the headless and hanging bodies were left in the square for days before their families were allowed to retrieve them for burial.

The Christian population had good reason to fear. The execution of their leaders could have been a preamble to a general massacre, a method which had been previously used to control the subjects of the sultan. Thus, the people remained subdued and quiet in the face of the horrors and threats that they were facing. They needed, much against their true feelings which burned for liberty, to reassure the Ottoman authorities that they were nothing more then the loyal subjects of the sultan. Submissiveness was the only realistic response to an overwhelming and tyrannical power that could unleash unopposed, unlimited terror on the defenceless people.

Gradually, the fear of rebellion died down and the blood lust of the masters was allayed. Thousands had been massacred while others fled west to the safety of the Ionian Islands. Eventually, new church leaders were selected who swore loyalty to the sultan and life began to return to normal. The people resumed their everyday preoccupations as shop keepers, artisans, as farmers tilling the soil, sowing the seed and harvesting the produce of the earth and despite the hardships of life, they worshiped steadfastly in their Orthodox Christian faith, giving thanks to God for all that they received.

~

The reaction of the Ottoman authorities had been swift, bloody and brutal. So much Greek Cypriot blood had flowed even when it was clear that the population was totally at the mercy of the heavily armed Moslems and were in no position to carry out any acts of resistance. Such a blood thirsty reaction surely sowed the seeds of distrust and hate between the Greeks and Turks of Cyprus that would one day germinate into renewed bloodshed.

If only the Ottoman authorities on the island had had the imagination and intelligence to use reason and not massacre as a tool for controlling the political crises and putting an end to any aspirations of union with as yet non- existent Greek state, the tragedy would have been avoided. Instead of unleashing a reign of terror upon the defenceless Greek Cypriots, Kuchuk Pasha might have tried to be more diplomatic and more persuasive. If only he had used wisdom and not terror then the modern history of Cyprus might have been very different. One can only imagine the speech that a wiser and more diplomatic Turkish leader might have given to the Cypriot people:

"People of Cyprus, Greek Christians have rebelled in the Moria where they have declared war on the Sultan and the empire. They have massacred their Moslem neighbours and have declared their independence. The army of the Sultan even now is marching to crush these rebels, Inshallah. As for you, do not make the mistake of thinking that you can join the Greek rebels of Moria. Cyprus is very far away from Moria and you are cut off from their forces which in any case are weak, disorganised and, as will be soon proven beyond doubt, very ineffective. And why should you join these people of whom you have no idea about, against the Ottomans who have done so much for you? Allow me to remind you of some events in our history. It was the victorious Ottoman army that drove out the hard and uncompromising Catholic Venetians who kept you in a state of serfdom, no better than slaves. The Sultan made you into free men and granted you land ownership. He granted your church rights above the Catholic Church and for your Archbishop the position of Ethnarch of the people was created. People of Cyprus do not be so foolish as to endanger the loss of all that you have gained with the Ottomans for a vague dream that has been put into your heads by some misguided adventurers who have encouraged you to think that you can break away from the empire and be a part of some motherland that does not exist in the real world."

Such an approach would not have prevented rebellion amongst the Greek Cypriot population because such an undertaking was beyond their capability. But it might have had the effect of cementing a strong bond of friendship between the two communities through which a sense of fairness and justice would have allowed them to build a common future. Alas, it was not to be. The history of modern Cyprus is full of policies of confrontation and lost opportunities to achieve peace and stability for all its people.

The oppression and massacre of the defenceless Greek Cypriots in 1821 had without a doubt led to their reluctance to think of Turkish Cypriots as fellow Cypriots. The crumbling of the British Empire after the Second World War should have led to the unity of the two communities in a struggle for independence. Instead, the seeds of mistrust and fear that had been sown by the massacres of 1821, led the Greek Cypriots to seek greater security in a union with Greece and for the Turkish Cypriots to oppose such an outcome by joining forces with the British to fight against Greek Cypriot aspirations while pursuing their own policy to partition Cyprus.

It is clear that the bloodshed of 1821 has led to further bloodshed in the 20th Century. The lesson to be learnt by the two Cypriot communities, even at this late stage is that with a little more compassion and understanding , with more enlightened political attitudes, much can be done to heal the wounds from the past.

~

Some years after the execution of the Ethnarch Archbishop Kyprianos, news arrived and spread like wild fire across the island: Greece had gained its liberty, Greece had become a state. This sudden and dramatic news rekindled the hope that one day Cyprus could also gain its freedom but for the moment Cyprus remained under the oppressive Ottoman rule until the coming of the British, which would not be for another fifty years. Ironically, during the First World War, the British were to offer Cyprus to Greece in return for Greek support in the Balkans. The Greeks declined but later, nevertheless, entered the war on the side of the British. They had, however, lost the opportunity of gaining Cyprus and the offer was not to be repeated. There was a failure in the political understanding of the Greek state. Greece had failed to comprehend that it was never in a position to gain what it wanted or to become what it aspired to be. It had foolishly turned down the only time when it was actually possible to gain the island perhaps under some kind of mistaken illusion that this could be achieved at some later date.

The sad reality for Greece is that it is a small country with limited military and economic means and in most situations would not be able to compete with the more powerful predatory powers around her borders. This failure to comprehend harsh realities led to the catastrophe in Asia Minor during 1919-1923 when thousands of Greeks lost their lives and more then two million Greeks of Asia

Minor were forced to abandon their homes in the new Turkish Republic and to resettle in Greece.

As if such a national catastrophe was not enough, the Greek state against all logic attempted to gamble with the fate of Cyprus without taking into consideration that the other players in the game held much more powerful hands and that the future of Cyprus would be put into jeopardy. In 1974 Greece predictably lost the game and Cyprus paid the heavy price of having one third of its territory occupied and 200,000 of its people made refugees in their own home land. Unfortunately, there is no end as yet to the saga of the Cyprus tragedy and the people of the island continue to struggle for a just settlement that seems both remote and unlikely.

~

Father

In 1956 my father decided, like many other Cypriots, to immigrate to England in the hope of building a better future. The economy of Cyprus during the 1950s remained stagnant and backward. There were few opportunities for ordinary people to improve their standard of living. The majority of the population lived in poverty without any real hope of a better future. The United Kingdom at this time was under going an economic boom. The country was rebuilding and re-modernising. Industry was working at full capacity and it needed a bigger labour force. People came from all parts of the empire to feed the demands of industry, the health service, the transport system. They came from India, the Caribbean, from Africa and they also came from the towns and villages of Cyprus.

Mother did not link the poverty that we suffered with any historical phenomenon. As far as she was concerned the present was enough to think about. She blamed father for our predicament because she knew that had he built a house in Sotira life would still not be entirely without problems but we would have managed. We would have had our own house; father was a craftsman, a shoemaker so he could have had some kind of income from that. He stood to inherit some plots of land that he could have cultivated, growing vegetables and potatoes for the market in Varosi. When mother thought about what could have been, she would bitterly admonish him. Father remained unrepentant.

"I am not going to labour in the fields to be scorched by the sun just to make a few *rials*. And I didn't want to stay in that dusty village with its uncouth people. I want to go to England. At least there I can find employment and live like a man. It will be better for all of us, believe me."

"If you don't have enough sense in your head to build a life in your own country how will you do it in a foreign land?" mother answered, unconvinced by his shallow argument.

"Many men are going to England!" my father shouted back. "They are not afraid and their wives are happy and give them encouragement. I will go first, find a job, a place to live and then you and the children can join me. What's wrong with that? But all you can do is moan at me. We need to do this for our children."

Mother looked at him feeling uncomfortable and uncertain by his proposal. To leave Cyprus, her parents, her sisters, her familiar world to go to England where she could not even speak the language and with a husband who was not totally reliable seemed to be a gamble in which she would be a certain loser.

~

My father came to England with a family who had lived in a baranga next to ours in Varosi: Kalisteni, her husband Prokopis and her children Thomas, George and Anna. They came together to an address and to jobs that had already been arranged for them. Mother had spent what little money she had to buy father a new suit, some new shirts and a new tie. Carrying a suitcase in one hand and a bag containing his shoe maker's tools in the other, he arrived at Victoria Station. It was on the evening of 27th January, 1956.

In later years he often told the story of an incident that occurred just after getting off the train. He would describe the occurrence with some amusement, probably at the thought of his own naivety. At the time, he took it to be a sign of the good fortune that he would find in this new land of hope:

"I'd just got off the train. There were hundreds, thousands of people all around. This was London, the greatest city in the world and I'd never seen so many people in one place before. My long journey was over and I was ready for my new life in this great city. As I made my way out of the station, I looked down and there and in front of me I saw a wallet that had been dropped by some unlucky person. I felt too proud to pick it up. I smiled, thinking that in this land people were not so desperate and that I would have better fortune just around the corner."

It wasn't long before he realised that the years ahead would be difficult and that progress could only be achieved with sacrifices, even in England. His passport stated his name: Loizos Pieris Loizou. His date of birth was the 5th of November, 1923 and that he was a citizen of the United Kingdom and Colonies. At the time of arrival he was thirty three years old. The photograph in his passport showed a handsome and well dressed man in the prime of life, a man who might engage with the struggle against poverty and who might succeed.

When my father came to England in search of a better future, he was following other Cypriots who had immigrated to England even before the war. Like all refugees, they shared the same dream. They wanted to find a place of safety, security, to work, to build some kind of prosperous and worthwhile life. And so my father followed in the footsteps of the refugees; the hundreds of thousands, the millions who have always existed in our world, crossing oceans and continents like migratory birds in search of new nests.

~

The tide of Cypriots coming to England coincided with political problems and bloodshed on the island. In fact, economic stagnation, unemployment, poverty and the outbreak of political violence had all greatly contributed to the decision of thousands of Cypriots from all backgrounds to leave their motherland and to seek a home else where.

The political crisis had come again to the boiling point in 1955. The aspiration for union with Greece had been supported even by the British during the First World War but had been rejected by Greece. It was, therefore, reasonable to assume that given the right circumstances the goal of Enosis could somehow be achieved.

The young people of Cyprus had answered the call to arms to fight alongside Britain and its allies against Nazism and Fascism in Europe. Thirty thousand Cypriots fought as members of the British Army. They fought and some died in the belief that Cyprus would in due course be united with Greece. In 1940 Greece was the only country in Europe which was actively engaged in the war on the side of Britain.

After the war the Cypriots felt that the union with Greece should be granted. The church encouraged this political aim and in 1950 a plebiscite engineered by the young and energetic Ethnarch Archbishop Makarios 96% voted in favour of union with Greece. This was not a new political sentiment. The Cypriots had tried to align themselves with the 1821 war of Greek independence but they were geographically too far from the Aegean to be supported and had been brutally crushed by the Ottomans. In 1931 there were ferocious riots in support of Enosis. The burning down of Government House had led the British to suspend the representative council of the Cypriots. The British Government now seemed determined that Enosis should not be achieved.

Another factor which quite erroneously was not contemplated by the Greek Cypriots and their leaders was what the response would be of the Turkish Cypriot community and of Turkey itself to the demands for union with Greece. It should have been apparent to the Greek Cypriots that though union with Greece might have been their nationalistic dream, it was a dream too difficult to achieve even though they made up eighty percent of the population because Turkey was powerful enough to prevent its realisation. The geographical distance from Greece and the proximity to the Turkish mainland added to the immense difficulties of achieving Enosis and these are the same reasons why Cyprus was defenceless and did not play any significant role in the Greek War of Independence.

~

The Teddy Boys

My father arrived in London just after the EOKA* campaign had begun in Cyprus on 1st April, 1955. Not long after, when EOKA had started to gun down British soldiers or personnel, the Cypriots in London, not surprisingly, had suddenly become very unpopular with the local people. There were racist attacks on individuals. Cypriots were offensively called "bubbles". They became the focus of attention of the " teddy boy" thugs who used any excuse to intimidate, insult or physically attack innocent immigrants including the Cypriot`s who had left Cyprus to avoid the uncertainties of their strife torn island but who were now seen as enemies of Britain. My father spoke of the occasion when he and Kalistenis' sons had to arm themselves with pieces of wood and knives just to be able to make it out of the estate where they were living, in Kings Cross. They could only come and go in a group for mutual protection, otherwise, they would have become the easy prey of the marauding teddy boys.

"The teddy boys would gather at the entrance to the flats. Most of them were only sixteen or seventeen year olds. They didn't really understand the seriousness of what they were doing. They probably enjoyed wearing their teddy boy clothes and combing their hair like Elvis Presley. They would loiter around and make a lot of noise but they were not a great threat. It was only when they were joined by two or three older thugs who could be armed that things became really serious. Their tactics were usually to attack a person on their own or perhaps two people walking together. Their gang would be five or six in number and they often beat their victim severely so that he needed to go to hospital. On rare occasions people died. The police always arrived too late to apprehend any one involved in the attack. They would hit and run. Within a day or two they came back, loitering around, making a great deal of noise and looking for their next victim. There were four of us: Kalistenis three sons and me. They made remarks at us on our way in and out of the estate but there were enough of us to make them think twice about attacking us. We had to be very careful not to be caught alone by these thugs, otherwise it would have been very dangerous."

Once when father was relating this particular story, I asked him why he stayed in England if life was so difficult.

"I stayed because I had nothing to go back for. I had no work, no money and no home. The friends and companions were always fun to be with but they would not feed you or pay your bills. Above all you need work to earn money. Without this you are lost and England has mountains of work. You can work for the rest of your life and you will still have more work if you want it. That is why I have stayed here."

"What about the teddy boys and other racists?" I asked.

"The teddy boys were just a passing phase. The racists are always there and they are in every country. They are even in Cyprus where the Greek racists teach their children to hate Turks and the Turkish racists teach their children to hate the Greeks. Racists are everywhere and if you give them a chance they can destroy democracy. In England there are powerful people who will not let this happen. They are the same people who beat Hitler and the Nazis and they are not about to let some racist thugs destroy the democracy of this country. "

Despite his lack of education and some of his wayward habits, father seemed to have sound ideas in his head and it was when he spoke with such faith and optimism, despite so many challenges and problems in his life, that I sometimes felt very proud of him.

However, the racist attacks grew in intensity and by the summer of 1958, the West Indians living in Notting Hill were deliberately targeted by teddy boys and right wing racist thugs whose slogan was "keep Britain white". Eventually the sustained intimidation and attacks led to the Notting Hill riots in which West Indians confronted the teddy boys on the streets of that area. Some years later gangs of skinheads subjected the Bangladeshi community of Brick Lane to violence and abuse. Before these more recent arrivals to the shores of the British Isles, it was the Jews who had sought sanctuary from the pogroms of central and Eastern Europe, who in the 1930s had to face Mosely and his Fascist thugs dressed in black shirts in imitation of their role models, the German Nazis.

Obviously, even with an optimistic out look, it took sometime for Britain's new people to be accepted as citizens and for these new people to acquire the understanding of 'Britishness' that enabled them to become in their own right British people. This eventually happened, but it was then a distant goal that neither British people were aware of, nor the immigrants who had come to live amongst them. It was a gradual process of which the teddy boys and the Notting Hill riots, the attacks by skin head National Front supporters on the Bengalis of the East End and the provocative demagogy of

Enoch Powell represented those elements that rejected a society that could include people of different races, colour and creed.

Opposed to the racists was the concept of democracy held by reasonable people that all citizens are equal. Equality and equal opportunities for all groups in society was something that had to be worked on and achieved. It didn't happen on its own. There were people and politicians in England who were determined that it should happen. Most politicians understood that it was important for people in the United Kingdom to be treated with equality and dignity and they expressed this view in political debates. More marvellous then this, however, was the reaction of the ordinary British people who over a period of time showed that they could progress from the suspicion and sometimes hostility towards immigrants of the 1950s and 1960s to the understanding and appreciation of people from diverse backgrounds in this present time. Time, experience and goodwill, it seems, are good teachers.

At the end of his anecdotes about the teddy boy thugs, father had the habit of pausing to reflect upon what he had said. After a few moments when he seemed lost in his thoughts he concluded by saying,

"Most of the teddy boys were just silly, misguided teenagers. They were impressionable and behaved without thinking. Generally people were fair. You encountered these people in the street and in the work place. They were often busy getting on with their own lives, they had their own concerns and troubles. Most of the time they just passed you by without so much as a glance in your direction. The nice thing about the English is that they mind their own business most of the time and they expect you to do the same."

~

Only once did my father manage to post money to assist mother with her preparations for us to join him in England. Following is the letter that he wrote on that occasion:

London,
December, 1956.

Beloved wife,

    First, may I enquire regarding your health and the health of our children. I pray to God that you are all well. Praise be to God that I am well and am able to work every day and believe me, I am working day and night. My place of work is a factory that produces sausages and when you come to England their will be a job there for you also.
    At the moment I am living with our former neighbours from Cyprus, Prokopis and Kalisteni. They are good people and we try to support each other.

    It has been very difficult to save money because here in England, even though you have the chance to work and earn money, everything is very expensive and all the money soon disappears. You just would not believe how much it costs to buy a packet of cigarettes. It is three times what they cost in Cyprus.

I have saved some money and I am able to at last send to you £20 to help you with the preparation for your journey to England. Book immediately and without hesitation. I have already spoken to a certain Cypriot who has a large house and he is prepared to rent us two rooms and a kitchen. There is a good school nearby for Fotaki and also a secondary school for Kika because children must go to school until the age of fifteen. Everything will be ready by the time that you and the children arrive. We will work very hard and we will build our lives again.

London is a great and wonderful city. It is a huge place with thousands of streets lined with buildings stuck together on either side. Something that you can hardly believe even with your own eyes are the hundreds of trains that travel under the ground all day long carrying millions of people to work every day. There are really great opportunities in England and I know things will be better for all of us.

I miss you and the children, kiss them for me. That is all I have to say at this time,

Your husband,
Loizos.

Immigrants like my father who had made the journey to England or to the United States or perhaps to Australia did so with the intention of helping those who were left behind, usually the wives and children. In many cases money was sent to help maintain the families, paying for a son's secondary education or for medicine for elderly parents. Often, as in our story, the husband would be followed to the new land by the wife and the children.

*E.O.K.A. - Ethniki Organosis Kiprion Agoniston. (National organisation of Cypriot fighters) This was a military organisation that fought the British Army during 1956-1959. It was lead by Colonel George Grivas. Its aim was to unite Cyprus with Greece. This objective was entitled "Enosis" which simply means "union". The political struggle for Enosis was headed by Archbishop Makarios who gave his support and encouragement to Colonel Grivas and E.O.K.A.
It must also be said that at that time, the vast majority of Greek Cypriots who represented 82% of the islands entire population, supported the movement for Enosis. In my opinion Enosis was never a viable objective. It was doomed to failure because neither Britain nor Turkey were prepared to let it happen. The failure of the Greeks and Greek Cypriots to understand their political and military limitations led to the Turkish invasion and tragic events of 1974.

The Departure

By 1957 mother had managed to save enough money and with the small amount sent by father she was able to pay for our passage to England. We booked our passage through one of the few travel agents of that time. "Patsalidis" had a reliable reputation. We would travel by ship from Larnaca to Genoa in Italy and from there by overnight train to Calais. We would cross the English Channel to Dover and then complete our journey by train to Victoria Station.

My mother felt rather nervous at the thought of what was to her a long and complicated journey with two small children. Having to go by ship across the seas and trains that travel through countries where the people spoke in strange languages seemed very daunting to her. She had never travelled by ship or train before. She had never left the shores of her native island and so the prospect of what appeared to her an epic journey into very unfamiliar territory left her feeling somewhat anxious and a little nervous.

"Mr. Patsalidis, it seems a very long way and we don't speak their languages, I will be lost with my children."

Mr Patsalidis was a thin, wiry man in his late thirties. He was dressed in a brown summer suit and wore an eye catching shiny yellow tie. He sat on a wooden chair behind his desk that was covered with some neat piles of papers. He constantly made sharp, quick movements that are typical of people who are unable to relax and who should busily be getting on with things. He was reassuring because he had heard such doubts before.

"Don't worry, Mrs Loizou, there will be other people with you going the same way. Follow them and show your documents."

He smiled as he spoke to my mother who remained unconvinced by his smooth talking. He then suddenly paused, looked at mother in silence for a second or two, smiled again and as if he was able to see into the future, he remarked, "You will be fine, Mrs. Loizou, you will be fine."

Mother was as anxious as ever, but was still determined to make the journey.

The day of our departure was drenched in brilliant winter sunshine that gave the day a false sense of joy. Everything seemed in high definition, almost exaggerated as friends and family gathered at our baranga. They had come to say goodbye. My uncles Mihalis and Fotis with mother's sisters, their wives, Filou and Christinou had come with their children from Sotira to bid us farewell and to wish us success in our venture. Martha and her children with my grandparents, Kyros and Kyriacou, came from Stylloi.

In contrast to the cheerfulness of the morning my grand parents looked decidedly unhappy. They could not bear the thought that one of their dear daughters was about to leave with two of their beloved grand children, perhaps never to be seen by them again for who can say how life will evolve and what unforeseen circumstances may arise on life's journey. They were old and felt very uncertain about mother's decision to go.

The talking continued. Adults drank sweet Cyprus coffee in the shade cast by some pines and oleanders in the courtyard of the baranga. There were children playing and running around. There was laughter and encouragement. But the noise and light heartedness was transparent and only thinly disguised the fears and anxieties which were particularly felt by my grandparents. They knew that departure from the homeland was more permanent and often irreversible. There had been others who had gone to England or America; the years had passed by but they were never to return. Grandmother could no longer hold back her grief. There was an outpouring of hot tears that ran from her weather worn face. The chatter of adults and the children's games ceased as everyone present and with now serious, melancholic expressions turned their gaze towards the old matriarch who sat in the middle of her large family. She pleaded with my mother not to go.

"You will go to a far off land full of strangers, the bread of exile is bitter. Who knows what misfortunes await you... alone with your little children and an unreliable husband who will betray you; to whom will you turn?"

Her voice was filled with emotion. Grandmother mourned as if it was a funeral as she continued her arguments against the journey.

"You will be alone and isolated. At least here you are with people who love and care for you. In a foreign land who is going to look at you in your hour of need? Who is going to knock at your door to offer you even a crust of bread? Have you forgotten how your dear husband dragged you from Sotira to Stylloi and now from Varosi to only God knows where? Do not be fooled by him, he will never change, he will always betray you!"

Her tirade came to a sudden end. Grandmother's words had cut to the bone. She didn't care whether her words were hurtful or offensive. She felt that she was speaking the truth in an attempt to safeguard her daughter and grandchildren. She was determined that even at the eleventh hour she would prevent mother from committing what she believed to be the greatest mistake of her life.

Mother was moved by such an emotional expression of feelings but she managed to retain her composure and answered in a steadfast manner. She took her mother's hand, looked into her dark eyes, now reddened by her tears and spoke to her gently but with conviction.

"Mother, I must go to my husband; things will be better. What can we do here for our children? They can not eat the air. The young women grow old before their time and the young men waste their lives in listless unemployment. They become angry because they have no future. Do not worry mother, it is for the best, the children will have a chance in life. They will go to school, they will have a chance to become something wonderful and my husband and I will be able to work, we will have a home, a proper home, not a baranga like we have now. Our country is beautiful but for poor people like us the life is too hard! As for my husband, he has learnt from his mistakes and in his letters he promises that we will build a better life than what we had here. I have to trust what he says because he is my husband and the father of my children; one more thing mother, you know how scandalous Cypriots can be about a woman without a husband. They will start malicious rumours that I sleep with other men and very soon I will have a reputation of being worse than a prostitute. No, mother, I cannot permit such a thing to happen."

Mother had spoken with passion. It was an emotional outburst that she needed to express as if she was somehow justifying her actions not only to others but also to herself. However, mother's dramatic proclamation did not impress grandmother who then just busied herself with the children trying very hard for my mother's sake to weep no more. There were times, however, in the following months and years when mother expressed her feeling that she should have listened to grandmother's advice.

Just before we boarded the bus for Larnaca, we all sat down in a group for a photograph to be taken. At the front seated were my grandparents and I sat in between them. Behind us, arranged in two lines were my uncles and aunts. Many years after when I visited Cyprus I saw this photograph for the first time on the wall of my aunt Eleni's living room. The photograph held my attention not only because I saw myself as a little boy surrounded by the people who loved me but because the photograph had captured the moment after which the familiar life, that could have been, was to change for an unpredictable experience. The photograph captured the moment of sadness of those who were left behind; it showed the relationship that would imminently be severed but also of the hope of a better future for those who were leaving.

The suitcases were then hoisted onto the roof rack of the old, rusting bus. They contained all our belongings. Mother was careful to pack 'malina' woollen sheets for the cold English climate. These sheets had been woven at home by my grandmother who worried that we would not be warm enough in the winter months ahead. She had also packed towels, table cloths, knives and forks, some pots and pans beside our ordinary clothes. She had put into those suitcases as much of her household belongings as possible for her new home in England. Mother had also shared most of her household possessions between her sisters. She gave to them pots and pans of good quality, a fine, solid oak dining table with some chairs and an iron bed with a comfortable mattress. Many years after when I visited my aunties, they pointed to these things and commented on how generous my mother had been.

"This table and this iron bed belonged to your mother, Fotaki, and she kindly gave them to us."

Another aunt perhaps added some explanation on how it came about that she had acquired mother's household items,

"She gave me those plates with a fine glaze and the heavy cooking pots because you were going to England and she had no means by which to take them with her."

My aunts had always been kind and religious women but on those occasions when my mother's things were displayed before me, I was overcome with the uncomfortable feeling that my aunts had been happy to benefit from our departure to England. Perhaps, I was wrong about this and I was only disturbed with the thought that those things made us into merely a memory in the place where we should have had a real existence; but this was not something that I dwelt on for too long because the past is beyond our ability to alter so that we may take away the painful and sad events that might be uncomfortable for us in the present.

Just before we boarded the bus, my sister's best friends came to say good-bye. It was Eve, who was my sister's closest and dearest friend. Later, in England, my sister often showed the photograph of Eve and always commented that she was indeed a very beautiful girl, a charming person and a dear friend. Eve's brother was Kokos. He was a fine, handsome young man who had warm feelings for my sister and had hoped one day to make her his wife. After some years we had been in England, Kokos suddenly and unexpectedly turned up from nowhere, seeking my sister. He was shocked and upset to discover that she had become engaged to someone else and he left our house looking bewildered and despondent. Eventually, after years of being in England and because of the upheavals of 1974 in Cyprus, contact with such friends was lost. Information about old acquaintances was sometimes discovered through a chance meeting with a common friend who explained and told the story of what may have happened to those who were once close, with whom life would have been shared but with whom the bonds were severed by the decision to go far away across the sea to another land.

We eventually boarded the old rusting bus. From the windows we looked out at the scene. We looked at the baranga with its walls of peeling paint, its leaking roof and windows that did not close properly. This had been our home. The warm, winter sunshine, the azure dome of the sky and the tranquil, timeless, solitary caique that could be seen from where we were, sailing below the horizon in a sparkling sea was not enough to lighten the sombre mood. With tears and with brave smiles we waved good-bye to friends and family. The driver revved up the engine and with a sudden jerk the first steps of the journey were taken. The bus slowly wove its way through the narrow streets of Varosi, passed the old Venetian walls of the city and on to the road in the direction of Larnaca from where we intended to embark on a ship for Genoa in Italy, our first port of call. Little did we know then that the passing of time and the fortunes of war would mean that even up to this present moment we are prevented from returning to the beloved city of Evagoras, the place of my earliest memories, the place where I first went to school, where I played on its golden beach and where I first began to have a sense of myself.

The Journey

There was hardly any traffic on the road. The bus occasionally overtook a lonely cyclist or slowed down as it carefully went by a "carretta", a two wheeled cart used by farmers and usually drawn by a single horse. The countryside seemed still, silent like a painting of an Italian medieval landscape. The first indication that our bus journey was almost complete was when we saw the salt lake. The rain had been heavy at the beginning of that winter and the lake which was always dry in the summer months was now almost overflowing. There were flocks of wild birds that had migrated from Europe on their way to Africa basking and feeding in the warm waters.

Opposite, the far bank of the lake was covered with green shrubs and exotic palm trees. Amongst the deep green branches of the palm trees, almost hidden, we caught sight of the Tekke of Hala Sultan, the resting place of the Prophet's relative Oum Haram, who had fallen from her horse and had died there. The magical impression of the Tekke seemed to come straight out of the stories of the "Arabian Nights". In the years to come I would recall this scene in my mind's eye when thinking of my distant homeland.

The bus soon arrived at the port, outside the point of embarkation. As we alighted from the bus, a flock of birds swirled three times above the port and then flew off towards the open sea. They were migratory birds moving compulsively towards new destinations, to build new nests in far off places. They flew swiftly, slicing through the air, without hesitation or fear. They flew with a purpose and a certainty without the need to look back.

We stood on the quay looking out at the ship that was anchored some distance from the shore. There were at least fifteen or twenty other people who were also waiting to embark. There were men who were standing alone, with one or two suitcases beside them; perhaps some were single men without wives or children who were intent on finding their fortune. Others might have been bread winners with families to think about, who wanted to work hard to provide a better life for them. There were some couples who were holding hands tightly in case the one would leave on the ship without the other. Whatever their reasons for leaving their place of birth, they were waiting patiently for their turn to be transported to the waiting ship.

The port of Larnaca in those days was not sufficiently deep to allow ships to dock within it. Our several suitcases were loaded onto a small craft and then we also boarded. The sea was calm and turquoise blue. When we had settled, the engine was started up and the boat quickly cut through the clean water while its operator, a stout, unshaven, sunburnt man whistled and spoke in a loud voice.

"Don't be afraid, you're safe with me. So you are going to England! You'll all be rich very quickly. You'll be back before you know it with your pockets full of money."

He laughed loudly at his own irony while his passengers uncomfortably noted the depth of the water and how his little boat was heavily overloaded. Soon we came by the side of the ship and stopped where a rope and wooden staircase had been lowered to enable us to embark. We made our way on board and some sailors brought on our luggage. The ship was crowded with Cypriots on their way to England. Mr Patsalides was speaking the truth when he said that we would not be alone on this journey. As we stood on the deck we noticed that the smoke from the two funnels of the ship had increased and there was the rumble of the engines from inside the depths of the ship. Then it began to move, first very slowly, and then with greater speed. As I stood on the deck peering out over the railings, it seemed to me that the land was moving and that the ship was static. Gradually, the ship moved on leaving the shores of Cyprus far behind and out of sight.

At night, the passengers crowded on the decks; they took out blankets and made sleeping arrangements under the Mediterranean night sky. The air was fresh and cool and the firmament was lit up by constellations of stars. The people were joyful, as people often are when they set out on long journeys. They were full of hope and optimism for the future. They talked, laughed and engaged in serious conversations. Some were delighted to meet up with acquaintances, friends or relatives, all making the same journey. There was innocence, naivety in the expectations of these people. Many were from villages. They were shepherds or farmers, skilled in turning the soil, planting, irrigating crops, reaping the seasonal fruits of the soil. Those from towns were small traders with crafts: a tailor, a shoemaker, a carpenter or a barber. All were poor and all were immigrating for a better future. Their aim was to build something, to achieve, to find opportunities. All had a dream and a desire to improve them selves. England was the promised land: a land of hope, a land at the end of the rainbow, a land flowing with milk and honey. And for the majority, England would provide some realisation of their dreams. Whatever the distant outcome, the experience which began on that ship sailing through the night would change their lives in many unforeseen ways. The immigrants were leaving behind an ancient land

and even these simple people were full of its history, they knew its culture and practised its traditions. They breathed, spoke and felt their identity. They were Greeks of Cyprus, God fearing, Christian and Byzantine.

We too, met acquaintances and friends. George, my father's first cousin, was also travelling to England. He was a slender man in his early thirties. He had brown curly hair that was neatly cut and combed back to expose a broad forehead. His expression was serious but he had a friendly and polite manner. He showed great respect for family ties and it was our good fortune that through coincidence he was travelling with us. He proved to be our constant friend and helper. When my mother often repeated her thanks and expressed her gratitude to him for his assistance, he would smile and modestly say,

"It is for my relatives, we are one family, we are one blood."

He was a shy person but he was always with us, lifting or carrying some of our luggage or looking out for our safety, making certain that we were never in any kind of danger.

I was beginning to enjoy the journey; I was six years old and I had never been on a ship before. When I looked at the bow of the ship, how it sliced its way through the water, I was filled with excitement. On that very first day of our journey, we sighted dolphins swimming by the side and ahead of the ship, darting through the water, leaping and diving in and out of the sea. I was so excited running hither and thither to keep sight of them. My mother became so alarmed that I might somehow fall off the ship or have an accident that she forced me at all times to be with her. I felt restricted and my fun was again being spoilt. She held me by the hand and would not let me out of her sight. I stood next to her with a miserable expression on my face, feeling glum and sad at the level of motherly control I had to endure. Life seemed so very unfair!

On the second day of our journey, we sailed north of the island of Crete and onwards towards Italy. The adults would spend most of their time talking or perhaps resting in their cabins. There was actually little to do because, though the ship was transporting passengers, it was also a cargo ship engaged mainly for the purpose of carrying goods and therefore afforded little comfort to its passengers. For me, however, it was a magnificent sailing ship that was carrying me, as I imagined, on some great adventure and I pondered in my childish imagination whether we would stop on the island of the Cyclopes or perhaps encounter the Sirens with their mesmerising songs.

On the third day of our journey, we disembarked at Genoa. Italy was the first foreign country that we had ever been to and Genoa was like no other place that we had ever seen before. There were masses of people everywhere you looked. Some were dressed in very fashionable clothes, walking in a kind of slow promenade as if inviting on lookers to note their importance while others busily went about their affairs and all the time we could hear people engaging in the musical Italian tongue. Some were speaking in a loud tone as they walked along, others were calling out to each other, children laughed and talked at the same time. The sound of this language impressed and entertained us with its tone and its rhythmic qualities. Mother was very impressed with the Italian sense of style and the animated manner of the Italians. These Europeans were so different from the English people that she had worked with at Four Miles. The Italians with their dark hair and olive skin, their loud voices and body language seemed familiar people. She felt their warmth and could relate to them as if they were rediscovered, distant relatives.

"What beautiful buildings and the people seem to be so kind," mother occasionally uttered but her favourable opinion of Italy and the Italians was not destined to endure for any length of time: we had some spare time before our train was due to leave and so we went for a walk in a park, close to the railway station from where we were to begin the second stage of our journey. This particular park must have been a place for young lovers. After strolling for about five minutes, mother could no longer ignore what she was seeing .There were young couples on park benches or lying on the grass, embracing and kissing. Some were passionately and erotically grasping each other. Mother could not believe her eyes. She had never seen such things going on in public in Cyprus; she felt that this was an outrage and a great sin.

"This place is Sodom and Gomorrah," she cried. "God will punish this world."

In a panic, she grabbed my hand, ordered my sister not to look at what was going on, covered her eyes with her other hand and with a feeling of righteous indignation marched out of the park and straight to the train station where we remained until it was time to board.

"What kind of a place is this," she repeated, " in which women allow men to embrace them in public as if they are in the marriage bed?"

Her opinion of Italy and the Italians had significantly changed from her first impressions .

~

To my mother and to the Cypriot women of her generation, the codes of dress and behaviour were dictated by what was thought to be standards of decency. A woman, they felt, should always be serious in public; not to be flirtatious or loud. She should be dressed modestly and wear little makeup if at all. The model of womanhood that was adhered to was that of a well behaved daughter, a loyal wife or a noble mother. Anything else was considered unacceptable for an honourable family woman. Thus, most of the women journeying to England came from a deeply religious and conservative society in which roles were clearly defined; the boundaries between what was acceptable and unacceptable were drawn in clear bold lines.

The Cypriot women of the 1950s worked extremely hard, cared for the house, brought up children and they were very subservient to their husbands. As single young women, their only prospect was marriage. The family began the preparations for the daughter's marriage even before adulthood. They provided a dowry, a house, furniture and sometimes land. It was unusual for women of the 1950s to be educated beyond primary school or to be a member of a profession, apart from perhaps school teaching.

My mother, like the other women of her time, spoke of these circumstances and conditions but these women also felt proud of their allotted place as wives, mothers and even as possessions of their husbands. Sometimes, they suffered the brutality of domestic violence inflicted upon them by husbands who felt they had a right to do this. Such men expressed the view that a woman should be kept in order. The Cypriot women of the 1950s did not openly rebel against such attitudes. They accepted them because it had been like that for their grandmothers and mothers; such was life ,they felt, and there wasn't anything that they could do about it.

~

It was late afternoon when we boarded the train in Genoa. The suitcases were large and heavy but thankfully George, my father's cousin, was there and was always willing to help. We soon found a compartment to ourselves, took out some bed clothes and blankets. The weather felt noticeably colder.

Eventually, the train set off and we were on our way, leaving the Mediterranean behind, heading towards France and beyond towards the English Channel. Mother was sitting between my sister and me. Opposite us there was George. We talked and laughed; we were all very excited that we were at last well on our way. There was relief that we had completed the first part of our journey. We had crossed the sea and with each passing moment we were travelling further and further from Cyprus and the world that was familiar to us. When would we again see its quiet, tranquil villages and sleepy little towns where the church bell tower stood side by side with the minaret? How were we going to feel when we would walk along unfamiliar roads, lost amongst people who spoke another language and who would look upon us with inquisitive glances?

The train seemed to be moving at a very high speed, faster then any vehicle that we had ever been on before. I could not sleep that night. I lay awake filled with a strange joy, sensing that our journey was the prologue to great changes in our lives. As I closed my eyes to sleep, I felt the powerful heart of the train beating rhythmically with enormous strength like some magical dragon from the fairy tales, breathing fire as it journeyed through the cold darkness of the night, across deep valleys and through dark tunnels barrowed into mountains, crossing plains and forests, drawing ever closer to our destination.

By mid-morning of the next day we had reached Calais. It was a rather cold and grey day with a drizzle that chilled us to the bone. There was no warm Mediterranean winter sunshine here! The demeanour of the people reflected the drabness of the environment; they were rather impersonal and to me they looked rather sad. They hardly ever looked at each other and seemed to be in a great hurry. They had pale, unsmiling faces that seemed almost expressionless. We were quickly and efficiently transported from the station to the port where we boarded the ferry for Dover.

Once we had eventually managed to put our luggage in a secure place we all went on deck to look at the scene. The sea had always been a familiar sight to us but what we looked upon was something quite different from what we were used to. The sky was a dome of light grey with patches of white. There was hardly a horizon, the grey sky blended with a grey sea while the cold, fresh wind from the North Atlantic made our senses feel vibrant and alert, giving us a sense of well being. We were further enthused when the greyness of the sky suddenly broke and in the distance, appeared a patch of blue through which bright silver rays from the hidden sun beamed towards the glittering sea. It was a tremendous, unfamiliar to us, panorama of delight. As we stood there on the deck of the cross channel ferry, taking in the scene of sea and sky, Uncle George pointed to the white cliffs of Dover.

"There, there is England!" He exclaimed in a voice full of excitement. The cliffs even from far away appeared to be gargantuan and majestic. They were like the walls of an impregnable fortress, guardians of England's liberty. I suppose we should have felt some kind of emotional excitement but we were as yet unfamiliar with the stories and events that had made the scene of the white cliffs so special for the English people.

After disembarking, we were again efficiently conducted to our train for the last part of our journey. Once on the train, I sat by the side of the carriage window looking out upon the scene. This was a neat, green land. The weather had changed since we were on board the ferry. The sun was now shining in a blue sky with small fluffy white clouds moving across it like little sailing ships on a blue ocean. There was field after field of rich green grass full of flocks of fat woolly sheep or herds of dappled black or brown milk cows, grazing on the luxurious grass. The train passed through towns with neat, two storey houses that were roofed with red or black tiles and where the steeples of little churches pointed high into the sky. Everything seemed so fresh, clean and crisp in the cold winter sunshine.

As we neared the great metropolis of London, the buildings were larger and the roads appeared more and more congested until all we could see were buildings, thousands of smoking chimneys, roads and motorcars. The clean, green countryside could no longer be seen. Everything was brick and mortar, iron or steel. Sometimes, we glanced at some grand church with a high steeple or tower with a clock surrounded by more buildings and roads. Occasionally we caught sight of buildings that had been destroyed by the German Luftwaffe and had not yet been rebuilt. These blackened ruins seemed odd in the middle of a bustling metropolis and, of course, we had no idea that they were caused by the bombs that rained down on the people of London during the dark days of the Second World War.

I became increasingly excited when the train approached and crossed a gigantic bridge that spanned over the dark, fast flowing waters of the River Thames with the defiant, majestic dome of Saint Paul's Cathedral and the Palace of West Minister along the margin of the river, basking in the hazy afternoon winter sunshine. The train was now moving very slowly as it began its approach to the station. On either side there were countless shiny, smooth rail tracks that curved and crisscrossed each other like silver, slithering, metallic snakes, fading into the mammoth mouth of some dark tunnel. There were static trains that seemed to be resting after long journeys and trains slowly moving in the opposite direction to us, beginning their journeys to the different towns and cities of the land. Eventually, we entered a huge structure that was made from a web of steel and covered with glass panels. As I sat with my forehead against the carriage window, awed by the brave new world that I was now entering, the train suddenly jerked and came to a complete standstill. Feeling tired but excited, we had at last arrived at London's Victoria Station.

London

We had been travelling for four days. We felt dirty and exhausted but we knew that we had at last completed the final part of our journey. We had arrived at our destination.

"Is it here, mama? Have we arrived? Is this London?" I called out excitedly to my mother, tugging at her sleeve.

"Will papa be waiting?" asked my sister in an anxious manner.

"Yes, yes, of course, papa will be waiting. Everything will be fine, we will soon see him," she answered in an uncertain voice.

Uncle George was meanwhile unloading the luggage from the train in his usual enthusiastic manner and even though he was a slender man, he never seemed to tire. We would often meet together in the future.

Father was waiting for us. We emerged from the train dishevelled, fatigued and disorientated. He ran towards us. We could at last see him coming through the crowds. He had not changed at all. He seemed fresh and happy as he hugged mother and then he kissed both my sister and me. I remember how he picked me up and looked at me in the eyes and said,

"You have really grown up, you are now such a big boy and you will soon go to your new English school."

We collected our luggage and made our way to the waiting car. The driver was Hambos, who had been a neighbour in Cyprus. We said goodbye to Uncle George who had been our greatest help throughout the journey. He was being met by someone else and had his own people waiting for him. We hugged and we kissed him because he was now not only a relative but also a very dear friend.

Victoria Station made an impression on me. It was such a huge structure, bigger than any building we had ever seen before, it was like a gigantic cathedral and it was crowded with people. Some were standing around in little groups looking excited, sometimes laughing in an exaggerated manner and constantly engaged in conversation, others stood on their own waiting for their trains. There were crowds of people who sat in cafes reading newspapers or talking with each other while the waiters and waitresses busied themselves with cleaning the tables, taking orders and serving an endless stream of customers. Another crowd of men and women stood below a huge board and with concentrated, upturned faces reading the information on it. There were people of different races and some were dressed in colourful costumes from their native countries. There was a plethora of different people, talking and laughing, walking slowly or rushing about, men and women young and old, rich or poor; they were a mass, a crowd of humanity going about their lives each with their own private thoughts, a river of people that flowed in and out of the huge entrances and exits of the gigantic station. I looked on with the wonder of a child in a new, unfamiliar and bewildering world. Hambos, the driver, and my father picked up the heavy luggage while mother, my sister and I carried some small bags. We slowly walked through the crowds of people and made our way out of the station through a massive arched gateway. We walked through it then down some steps and onto the bright, busy and bustling streets of London.

As we drove through the roads on our way to our new home, everything seemed to be illuminated in a festive manner. There were lights from every building and from every window. There were shops full of goods on display and, despite the exhaustion we felt, we looked on, feeling impressed and delighted. In fact, we had become so engrossed with the scenes unfolding before us that we had hardly noticed the severity of the cold. It was a frosty winter's evening and unlike anything we had previously experienced. The pavements were crowded with people. There were young couples walking hand in hand or in each others arms laughing and talking at the same time. Older ladies held their companions by the arm while walking in a more dignified manner. Children held on to their parents' hands, skipping along by their side with upturned faces, no doubt asking endless questions. Everybody wore long over coats, hats and scarves. Some were carrying umbrellas; they walked on the pavements with a brisk pace as if they all had somewhere very important to go. I looked on from the inside of the car not believing that I was in the same place as the pedestrians a few feet away. Perhaps, my mind had not yet adjusted to my new environment; perhaps I felt that if I blinked my eyes I would find myself back at the beach in Varosi.

Our car journey took us from Victoria Station to Dalston. East London had always been traditionally the first port of call for immigrants coming to London. Father had rented two rooms and a kitchen in a house that was owned by a Cypriot couple. The terraced Victorian houses of Southgate Road seemed like castles to me. They had high brick walls and starting from the basement were three storeys high. The iron railings at the front were painted in black and had points like spears. The front door of our house was painted black like the railings outside and it seemed huge in comparison to the front door of our baranga.

We entered the house in some suspense, not knowing what to expect. Inside, we stood in a long, wide, dark passage leading to a stairway that went both to the upper floor and down into the basement. Beyond the staircase there was a door that led to the back of the house which was used as a kitchen. This huge house with carpets and electric lighting, with so many rooms was bewildering and strange. Our baranga had only two rooms and grandmother's house had no staircase or electric lighting.

"Is this where we are going to live, mama?" I asked repeatedly.

"Is this where we are going to live?"

"Yes, my dear, this is where we are going to live from now on. This is our new home."

"But mama, when are we going home to Varosi? All my friends are there and I want to play with them. Mama, when will I see my friends again?"

Mother looked at me with a sad expression but made no attempt to answer my questions.

The name of our kindly landlord was Christos and his wife was called Christala. They had been in England for some years and were more established then the recent arrivals. They proved to be a very welcoming and kind couple. Once we were at home, there was a hot 'avgolemoni', egg lemon soup with boiled chicken to eat. The driver ate with us and after my father had paid him for his trouble, wished us goodnight and left. My sister and I were put to bed in one room. As I lay in bed feeling warm and comfortable, I could hear my parents talking quietly in the next room. Across our dark bedroom, my sister was already fast asleep. I was slumbering between sleep and wakefulness; everything that I had seen on that day of our arrival flashed through my mind: the great railway station with all its movement and noise of people and machines, the lights of the streets, the shops and the innumerable men and women wrapped in their overcoats briskly walking onwards to their destinations, appeared in the eye of my imagination. How strange it was now to find myself in a big, dark room with tall windows and a high ceiling, in a house unlike any that I had been in before.

Gradually, with the quiet voices of my parents talking into the night, perhaps planning and looking forward to a happier and more certain future, I succumbed to my tiredness and went to sleep.

~

Thousands of Cypriots during the 1950s and 1960s made their way to England. At the beginning, the usual means of the journey was by ship and train. Later, air travel became more accessible and people travelled to England by air. There were, of course, Cypriots in London who had arrived pre-war. It was the custom amongst them to gather together to exchange news, to give one another support. Thus, if one Cypriot managed to open a business he employed other Cypriots. In the restaurants, or in the rag trade 'sweatshops' the budding Cypriot business men employed their fellow Cypriots; often they were members of the same family or had come from the same village or, perhaps, from the same town. If you asked any of these people why they had come to England they said that they wanted to work, to build some kind of a future and even in those early days it was clear to many that to achieve their dream they needed to be engaged in business and to have their own house. From such simple beginnings many families, as the years passed were able to achieve a remarkable prosperity.

~

My mother and father began with the same dreams and aspirations. They worked extremely hard. Father found work in factories around Dagenham. Unlike many other Cypriots, he never tried or was never inclined to have his own business. It wasn't in his character to be ambitious. He never felt the need to accumulate money or property. It was more important for him to live for the moment. Mother worked in the rag trade. She worked normal working hours and often brought work home so that she could earn some extra money in the evenings. After some years, she bought a sewing machine. It was a 'Singer', an industrial, electrical model. She became a home worker. Bundles of pieces of dresses, blouses or other items of clothes were delivered from the factory. When they were sewn into finished garments they were collected. For each dress the machinist was paid a few shillings. The machinists worked at home, cleaned, cooked and looked after the children. They supported the endeavours of their husbands. Mortgages were undertaken, businesses were established and thus, the economic life of the community had its very humble beginnings.

The winter of 1957 was severe. It was often freezing at night and in the day the mixture of fog and soot from thousands of chimneys across London blended to create smog, a toxic mixture that was sometimes lethal to those that breathed it. Children and elderly people and those with asthma or other breathing complications suffered the most. The Cypriots often joked that in the lack of visibility, you could bump into a lamp post and say sorry. The fog or smog and the freezing cold had an immediate effect on me. We lived in freezing cold rooms with no central heating. I developed a cold and cough, my temperature soared. I was ill for about three weeks. It was the impact of coming from a warm Mediterranean climate to a cold, damp and polluted environment. It was the one and only time that I suffered in this manner. I suppose it was a question of acclimatising and this I did very quickly.

Lego

Before long, my mother, with the help of our landlady who could communicate fairly clearly in English, took me to the local primary school. It was De Beauvoir Infants & Juniors in Balls Pond Road, Dalston. This was just off Southgate Road where we lived. A little before my 7th birthday, I found myself in an English school and not understanding a word that was spoken to me. I suppose in a child's manner I was very impressed with this school. It was an old Victorian building with little concrete staircases for the children leading onto a big hall with shiny parquet flooring that smelled of polish. The walls in the hall and corridors were covered in framed prints of famous paintings. There were large displays of the children's work: pictures done in paint or in crayons of many colours. Some displays showed the use of numbers while others contained children's hand writing. The large busy classrooms were around this hall. I was very excited and I didn't need to understand the language to see that in my new classroom there were paints, sugar paper of every colour, colouring pencils, scissors and lego which was entirely new to me. There were toys and books full of brightly coloured pictures. I looked on in wonder; I had never seen anything like it before. I loved it, particularly because I could feel that the children and the adults appeared very friendly and warm towards me. I was encouraged to join in, to paint and draw, to build lego, to write the letters of the alphabet. It was with great pride that at the end of my first day at a London school I took home a picture that I had painted. It was supposed to be a sailing ship with a big square sail. The sea was a deep blue and the sun was in bright yellow.

The next day I couldn't wait to go back to school. My excitement was enormous. I had lost old friends with whom I roamed on the sandy beach of Varosi but I now realised, in my own childlike mind, that I had made new friends and that I was going to a school that was full of interesting things to do. On the second day of my new school, I began to speak some simple words of the language that I would learn quickly and eventually study and love.

"Ya wanna play football?" asked my new friend.

He was a little boy with fair, straight hair and bright blue eyes. He looked at me, smiled and held the ball up.

"Football," I said by which I suppose I meant "yes."

So we both went down the narrow staircase with the small steps designed for the convenience of infants and juniors and out on to the playground. We kicked the ball around, shouted and enjoyed ourselves as only little boys could. Within a minute or two, other little boys joined in our game. I played with them, kicking and passing the ball; it was as if I had always been with them, a friend from the beginning.

I had settled into my new school very quickly. My parents were both working and my sister began to attend a secondary school nearby. We were here and we had now begun the process of settling into our new lives. In fact, Cyprus and my old friends, the sandy beach at Varosi were now in the background but not forgotten. My Grandmother and the village seemed distant and far but despite the geographical separation the people who had been a part of our lives remained in our minds and sometimes we referred to them as if they lived just around the corner and would appear at any time for a quick chat. Meanwhile, I was captivated and entranced by my new world and particularly by my new school. Creative activity had sparked the desire to learn. I drew patterns and coloured them in. I wrote the letters of the English alphabet and spoke some words like "thank you", "please", "excuse me, Miss", "May I have..." and so on. However, not everything turned out to be as pleasant or as smooth as my initial experiences and I was soon to discover that in our new world there could also be hurtful and damaging events:

One day in class, I was playing with some lego. I had a box of white coloured lego and I was busy constructing a castle. While I was silently and seriously engaged in this activity, lost in the imaginary world of play, another little boy came and tried to take my box of lego away from me. I was beginning to feel more at home by now and more confident in my new environment. So I resisted.

"No! No!" I exclaimed. "No" was one of the few words that I had learnt.

While this was going on, I had noticed that the teacher, who was an elderly lady in spectacles, was looking at what was going on from the other side of the room. She stood still and stared at the tussle that had developed between the other boy and me. I was desperately holding on to my lego while the other boy was trying to wrench the box from me. Pieces of lego spilled onto the floor. I could see the angry expression on the elderly teacher's face. Her eyes were glaring as she began to move slowly and purposefully towards us. I had thought that she was going to stop the other little boy from taking the lego from me. When she had approached us, she firmly took my hand and allowed the other boy to keep the lego that I had been playing with. I had stopped struggling and looked up at her stern grey eyes and firm thin lips. She then roughly rolled up my sleeve and smacked me four or five times very hard on the bare arm.

"That will teach you to fight with other people for things that don't belong to you! Let that be a lesson to you!"

Her face was very red and her voice was full of anger. The smack on the arm had stung me but worse then this was my confusion. I was very bewildered because I had expected her to allow me to keep the lego and to take the other boy away. There was silence in the class as the other children stared speechless at me and at the angry teacher. Everything came to a sudden halt, activity ceased. The violence inflicted upon me had shocked them. Never before had they seen their kindly teacher behave in such a way towards a child in her class. The teacher then just walked away without saying anything else and carried on as if nothing had happened. I was left standing in the middle of the classroom, not understanding anyone, not knowing what to do and feeling the intense humiliation of a little child that had been wronged. I didn't cry and I didn't move. I remained standing in the middle of the room looking down at the scattered lego around my feet. Though in my childish mind I did not have an understanding of the meaning of justice I was, nevertheless, overwhelmed with the feeling of having been wronged. I had been treated unfairly, my sense of humiliation was intense; I felt hot, embarrassed and degraded but somehow I held back my tears. After perhaps a minute or so, a young assistant teacher approached me and spoke softly.

"Come on, let's go and do some painting."

Her voice was gentle and reassuring. I followed her to a table where she gave me some paints and brushes. I picked up the brush and dipped it into the paint. I was painting in silence and not wanting to look up at anyone. I felt the corners of my mouth turning down and my chin quivering but somehow I continued to hold back the tears as I carried on painting my picture. When I had finished, I stood slightly back and examined it with care. It showed a little white house with a green door. The sky above was a deep blue and was cloudless. The sun was a bright yellow with thick rays that extended to the ground. In front of the little house there was the figure of what appeared to be a woman with a long, black dress and a black kerchief around her face. Next to her, stood a man with a long, black moustache, wearing a vraka, traditional Cyprus baggy trousers and holding a matsuka, a long shepherd's staff. They both had smiling faces. I felt as if they were smiling at me. As I looked at this simple picture I began to have a child's understanding of the meaning and value of the life that we had left behind. I also realised with the same child's understanding that this new world that had initially appeared to be so wonderful, could also be unpredictable, unpleasant and unwelcoming.

When mother arrived home that evening, she asked me in her usual manner what I had been doing at school and whether I had enjoyed my day.

"Did you have nice day at school? Have you learnt some more new words in English? Come on, Fotaki, let me hear you talk some of this new language!"

She had developed the habit of trying to coax me into saying something in the new language that I was learning and remembering her lack of schooling, she felt proud that I was attending what she thought was such a good school with very caring teachers.

"Today I learnt how to say 'smack' but I don't know what it means. The other children were saying this word to me."

"Tomorrow you ought to ask your teacher the meaning of this word. She will explain the meaning, I am sure. What else did you do?"

"I played with some toys and something called lego but best of all I painted a picture of grandmother and grandfather."

My words brought a proud smile to her face.

"Perhaps, you will go to a great English university one day and become a gifted artist, then, you will paint beautiful pictures and earn a lot of money."

The smile on mother's face instinctively made me feel that I had been smacked by the very person that she had felt was kind and protective. My instinct told me that if she had known this, it would have made her feel terribly unhappy and so I smiled at mother and didn't say anything.

Strangers in a Foreign Land

In 1957, the EOKA struggle for union with Greece was entering a bitter phase. EOKA liberation fighters engaged the British forces on the island. British soldiers and interests became targets and often innocent people suffered both among the Cypriots and amongst the British. Feelings in Cyprus had reached fever pitch. The Cypriots felt betrayed by the British for whom they had fought in both world wars. The Greek nation had always been a constant ally of Britain. The Cypriots could not understand how the British now refused to grant an island which was predominantly Greek in every respect and had shown such loyalty to Britain, the right to its political aspirations to unite with "Mother Greece". There was encouragement in the past from the British that one day Cyprus would be granted this right. The offer had previously been made but was not taken up. During the Second World War, Prime Minister Winston Churchill was impressed by the heroic "Oxi" of General Metaxa, the Greek leader, given in response to the Italian ultimatum to surrender. This was followed by the remarkable Greek campaign in Albania during which Italian forces were defeated and pushed back. Churchill then hinted that the Cypriots would find fulfilment in their political aspirations for union with Greece but after the war when the issue of Cyprus was debated in the House of Commons, the aspirations of the Cypriots were ridiculed. In the cruel light of day, Britain's position was that it would never relinquish control of this strategically invaluable island; this was particularly so after Britain's humiliation in Egypt and loss of control of the Suez Canal in 1956. An amusing anecdote to these events is when Winston Churchill is said to have refused to have Cypriot currents as a part of the ingredients for his birthday cake.

Colonel George Grivas was the military leader of the EOKA campaign. The EOKA group numbered perhaps a few hundred combatants. They were well organised, daring and believed in the justice of their cause. They managed to tie down 30,000 British soldiers. Archbishop Makarios III was the political leader of EOKA and had become an internationally recognised figure, some would say of equal importance to Jomo Kanyata of Kenya, Dr Milton Nkruma of Ghana and perhaps a more grand comparison with Mahatma Ghandi of India. EOKA claimed that its cause was that of freedom and liberty against colonial oppression. But despite the independence of India and the humiliating withdrawal from Egypt, the British Government had not yet come to a full understanding that the decline of the Empire was spiralling out of control. It wanted to confront the independence movements in Africa and Asia. It failed.

Cyprus, however, was a very small country with less then half a million people. It was easier to deal with. The great British Empire was now like a toothless lion and with its last gasp was determined to hold on to at least this last remaining corner of its possession and so attitudes became polarised. The Cypriots could not see the harsh realities of world politics, that Cyprus was militarily of great value to British and western interest and that it had to be controlled and so they demanded Enosis (union with Greece) with almost total disregard for the political position of the Turkish Cypriot minority and how the British might use the Turkish Cypriots to dent the aspirations for Enosis of the Greek Cypriots. The British Government could not understand how this small nation of about half a million people could have the audacity to make such a demand from them.... so, on the day when the EOKA gunman Nikos Sampson who had been accused of the murder of Sergeant Carter and Sergeant Thorogood, two police officers stationed in Cyprus, was acquitted, the British press reported the story in an inflammatory manner with reference to Ledra Street as being "Murder Mile" and implying that Cypriots were cold blooded murderers. The usually cool, patient and moderate British public became incensed, abusive and violent by the news reports. The explosive headlines had succeeded in their provocation which, in turn, resulted in teddy boy attacks against innocent Cypriots on the streets of London.

~

It is possible that the elderly teacher who had probably read the news story on her way to work, of how the callous Cypriot murderer of Sergeant Carter and Sergeant Thorogood had escaped justice, felt a great indignation at such a miscarriage of justice and perhaps, unthinkingly vented her anger on the little innocent Cypriot boy in her care who for historical and economic reasons had found himself in her classroom on that morning.

In the evening of that very same day, father was due to return home from work at his usual time. Mother had prepared the evening meal and we had been waiting for the sound of the front door and for his familiar footsteps on the creaking stairs. He was a little late and it was not with his usual smile that he entered. We were shocked to see that he had been badly beaten about the face. His face was bruised and covered in blood; his eyes were black and swollen. As he staggered into the room, my mother let out a cry,

"My God, what has happened to you?"

She rushed to him and helped him to a chair. He tried to calm my mother down.

"I am not really hurt badly, I will be alright. Just clean the blood off my face with some hot water with a little salt in it."

He bravely smiled at my sister and me but his voice trembled and I could sense that he was quite shaken by his experience. As mother began to clean his wounds, he gave us an account of what had befallen him:

"It was after work. I was just standing quietly at the bus stop, near the end of the queue. There was no sign of the bus so we were all waiting. There were a few men there from the factory but I did not know them. Suddenly three men appeared. They were young, perhaps twenty five years old or so. They pushed in front of me but I did not say anything to them because I knew that there would be trouble. But all the time they were looking at me, staring hard into my eyes. Then one of them suddenly shouted, 'Why are you looking at me, you fucking Greek bastard! ' and at the same time all three of them attacked me, kicking and punching me to the ground. There was no one to help me. The other people at the bus stop moved out of the way not wanting to get involved, perhaps they were frightened; who knows why they stood to one side and allowed a fellow human being to be treated in such a way. After a few minutes the thugs ran off laughing and jeering."

He stopped talking for a moment and as we looked on we knew that he was not physically badly hurt but his dignity as a person had been dealt a blow. My mother was perplexed and frightened and because at that time there was no one to help or to reassure us, my parents felt isolated and unwanted.

"It was a mistake to come here," she said.

"We have put ourselves in great danger. In Cyprus we were poor but at least no one attacked us in the streets."

My father who had suffered the attack was on this occasion more calm and patient.

"Andriana," he said. "I know that this is a terrible thing that has happened but it will pass. The people who attacked me were just thugs. There are many good people here who want to be friends and who want to help. We are not going to run away with the first difficulty that we have."

"What about our children when they are going and coming from school? Are you certain that they will be safe or will we come home one day to find that they have been attacked and beaten by these cruel people, like the ones who have attacked you today?"

By now mother's emotions had overwhelmed her and tears began to flow from her eyes and her face that was filled with an intense, troubled expression of sadness. My father stood up and gently put her in his arms in a reassuring manner.

"They would not dare touch children. The law is very strong here and such a thing would not be permitted to happen."

These were brave words from father which failed to convince mother because she kept repeating that we were no longer safe. Her fear was turning into a panic.

"We are in danger," she kept repeating. "They will harm the children. We are in danger. We are not safe here. These people don't want us here. We should go back to Cyprus, at least there, nobody bothered us."

"Calm down," my father implored. "You will frighten the children even more. It has been a very bad day and we will get over it, now please, stop crying."

Just then the electricity switched off and we were immersed in darkness. Father was flat broke and did not even have any pennies to put into the electricity metre to give us at least the comfort of some light. The only thing left to do was to go to bed. We were frightened and intimidated, cold and without light. Through that night I could hear my mother gently and quietly crying.

"What will become of us....what will become of us in this place....I want to go home ..."

My father did not reply.

The traumatic events of that day had made us feel like unwanted strangers in a foreign land and it was from then on that I began to have a sense of my otherness, that I was not entirely like other children and that I did not belong. I had been smacked at school by my teacher for a reason that I did not understand. My father had been attacked on the street on his way home from work. My mother had shed tears of fear and anxiety that my sister and I would come to some harm on the way home from school. How could we and other people like us, with similar experiences, not feel persecuted and unwanted?

Guy Fawkes

A few days before the 5th of November I decided that I was going to make a "guy" and collect some money to buy fireworks. I must have been eight or nine years old. The gun powder plot was celebrated in a big way in England and junior schools focused on this festival. The children studied the history of the Stuarts and drew pictures of Guido De Fawkes surrounded by kegs of gunpowder. My class room was transformed into a hive of activity. Some children painted a fireworks display with a splash of red, orange, yellow and white colours. Other groups of children were drawing and colouring in the portrait of the great conspirator who had plotted to blow up the Houses of Parliament. Other children wrote stories or were reading about how the plot was discovered in the nick of time and Parliament was saved from the Catholics, the terrorists of that time.

The story of the Catholic conspiracy interested me. In class, I drew my own picture of Guido De Fawkes. It showed him wearing a huge, high, black hat. I drew him with a black pointed beard and prominent black eye brows. When I had finished the picture I felt very proud of myself. Drawing and colouring was one area in which I was as good as the other children because it did not require the use of language with which I was still only a beginner. Despite this I was eager for my teacher's approval because I wanted to feel as good and as able as the other children who were constantly receiving praise and rewards. I took my drawing of Guido De Fawkes and ceremoniously presented it to my teacher who was sitting at his desk at the front of the class. He took one look at my picture, stood up to attract the attention of the class and with an artificial laugh exclaimed in a loud voice,

"Why, he looks like that terrorist fellow from your country....you know that Archbishop Makarios or whatever his name is, who is always trying to blow up our soldiers. He is just like him."

The other children laughed probably at the mocking humorous tone of his voice but I did not know whether to join in the laughter. I was confused by my teacher's reaction. I had expected some praise. He had always been a very kind man who often smiled at me in an encouraging way. I was not sure why he now spoke in that manner and why everyone was laughing at my picture. I stood at the front of the class looking from my teacher's grimace to the laughing faces of the other boys and girls. I couldn't understand why they were laughing; I was confused. Should I have joined in the laughter? Were they laughing at me? The teacher's face had become like a malevolent mask wearing a hostile grin. The faces of the other children were all turned towards me. They were laughing in an uncontrollable manner as if they could not believe that their noise was not being challenged by the teacher and were desperate to make the most of this moment of freedom. They continued to laugh and jeer at me, they were yelling words that I could not comprehend but felt that they were mocking me. I felt yet again, humiliated in the classroom. I was a spectacle while all around me was a sea of hostile faces. The teacher then handed me my exercise book and indicated with a motion of his head that I should sit down. I took my book and with downcast eyes I walked slowly back to my desk. I sat rigidly without looking at any one.

Gradually, all the noise ceased and the class resumed its normal activity without anyone paying further heed to me. I looked down at my drawing of Guido De Fawkes with the kegs of gunpowder stacked up all around him and with a lighted torch in his hands. What did my teacher mean when he said that my picture looked like that "Makarios fellow?" I was made to feel that I had some how done something quite bad and so I took up my pencil and drew lines across my drawing until it had been totally defaced.

Looking back on this incident, I can only conjecture that my drawing reminded the teacher of Archbishop Makarios because of my Greek Cypriot ethnicity and that his anger was aroused because Makarios, just like Guido De Fawkes, was responsible for acting against The Crown. If such is the explanation, then I do not feel that this particular individual would have understood the argument that it is right and proper for people to struggle and fight for liberty and independence from foreign rule. At the time, however, I had no inkling of what was going on.

Fireworks

I must have been a resilient little chap because I soon pushed this unpleasant experience to the back of my mind. I was determined that like other children I was going to celebrate Guy Fawkes Day and nothing was going to deter me.

One of the first rhymes that I learnt in the English language was the chant of Guy Fawkes:

> "Please do remember
> The 5th of November,
> Gun powder, treason and plot! "

My friends at school had already collected masses of fireworks for the occasion. Some of my friends brought them to school hidden in their bags to show the rest of us what they had collected. I had never seen fireworks before so I was very excited and I desperately wanted to buy some to join in the celebration. I looked at fireworks on sale in shop windows. I had learnt the names of the different varieties. There were bangers and Spinning Catherine Wheels, crackerjacks and sparklers but best of all were the rockets. They came in a variety of sizes, ranging from the very small to the very large and expensive. I looked on but in the back of my mind I remembered how my parents had said that we had no money for fireworks, they were too expensive and that I was not to go on the streets and ask for money for the purpose of buying fireworks.

"Fotaki," my mother said, "I don't want you to go anywhere while we are at work. I have seen those boys begging for money on the streets. Don't dare to do such a thing because I will be very angry with you."

"Mama, the English boys are not begging," I argued. "They are collecting money for the great festival of Guy Fawkes. They will buy fireworks with the money and they will have a great time. Why can't I do that?"

I wanted to persuade her by showing how much I had learnt about this subject.

"My teacher said that Guy Fawkes was a great Catholic terrorist who fought against the King. He was just like Makarios my teacher said. He put gun powder in the cellars of the Houses of Parliament but he was captured before he could light the fuse and they executed him by cutting off his head."

My mother looked astonished at what I was saying.

"I have told you, Fotaki," she now warned in a firm voice, "if you dare to go on the street and ask for money like a beggar and I find out that you have disobeyed my instructions you will be in serious trouble. Do you understand?"

"Yes, mama, I understand what you are saying," I answered with reluctance and without much conviction.

"And there is some thing else I want you to try and understand," she continued in a very serious manner.

"Makarios is not like the person you have described, he is not a terrorist. He is the Archbishop of Cyprus, he is very intelligent and he is fighting for the freedom of our country."

I didn't quite understand what she was talking about but I looked at her earnestly in the eyes and nodded as if I had fully comprehended her meaning and that I was in absolute agreement with her.

I had been given a stern warning by my mother regarding this matter but it was of no avail. So one morning, when they went off to work and my sister at that time was working in the same clothes factory as my mother, I got out of bed, quickly dressed and then began to construct a very odd looking Guy. I found an old pair of trousers and an old pullover. I tied the ends of the sleeves of the pullover and of the trouser legs with a piece of string and stuffed them with newspapers rolled up into balls. I crudely tied the torso and the legs together and then constructed a head with more rolled up paper upon which I stuck a round piece of cardboard with a smiling face drawn upon it. I then stepped back and looked at my construction. It must have been the most unconvincing model of a Guy in all the history of Guy making and I felt its limitations but I was determined to see my forbidden adventure through to its conclusion.

At that time we were living in Islington Green, before it had become "yuppified." Our house was situated in the connecting road facing Islington Green Park, linking Essex Road with Upper Street. On the far side going towards the Angel stood the statue of Sir Hugh Myddleton, an Elizabethan engineer, and on the opposite side, next door to our house, was the old Collins Music Hall which by then had been closed due to a fire. I took the odd looking Guy that I had constructed and placed him in a sitting position on the pavement, outside The King's Head, a pub across the road from the Rex Cinema.

It was fairly early in the morning and it was somewhat cold with a fresh wind. Most people who walked by just looked straight ahead, ignoring me, perhaps they were thinking of their work day and what was ahead of them. Some people smiled but hurried on and sometimes they smiled broadly and dropped a copper coin into the small box in front of my Guy. If my parents had seen me they would have most certainly been outraged at my disobedience and would have probably given me a smack or two.

It wasn't long before I had begun to accumulate a fair number of pennies and I was getting excited at the prospect of going to the local shop to buy some really good fireworks. I had seen a box on display with an assortment of fireworks in it. On the lid of the box there was a picture of Guy Fawkes with a little pointed beard, wearing a tall hat and carrying a lantern in his hand. It was just like the picture that I had drawn at school. This was the box of fireworks that I wanted and I was keen to make my purchase as soon as possible. I needed five shillings and sixpence in total but I did not as yet have this and so I stood there in the cold looking for the next passer-by who might provide an addition to my funds. Just then, from the corner of my eye I caught a glimpse of an unusual looking old man. He walked slowly in my direction and when he was fairly close I felt that he was looking piercingly at me. He was quite stout and well dressed in a smart suit. He wore a bowler hat which even at that time was quite rare and carried an umbrella that he used as a walking stick. He was neat, tidy and very red in the face. He kept his eyes on me but his face remained expressionless. I didn't know how to react. I felt uncertain whether I should venture to ask for a penny or perhaps look the other way and let him pass. When he was just a few feet from me, he looked at my Guy and sneered. I mistook this sign and thought it was some kind of a smile and so I briskly walked up to him like a playful terrier, full of confidence. I looked up and said,

"Penny for the Guy, mister?"

His reaction was cataclysmic.

"So you want a penny for the Guy, do you? You, fucking Greek bastard! Why don't you sod off back to where you come from!"

For a moment he stood staring down at me. His face was contorted; his left hand was clenched into a tight fist while in his other hand he had raised his umbrella like a club. I froze with fear. I stood still, motionless, as if my fear of this angry old man had immobilised me, as if I had been rooted to the spot where I had been standing. Suddenly, slyly, he looked right and left to check if anyone had been observing his hostility towards me. Without any further ado, he slunk off in the direction of the Angel, muttering something or other to him self.

These emotionally hurtful experiences were at the time bewildering. I knew that it was because I was from another land and it made me feel different. I was not like my friends at school and I felt as if there was something wrong with me. Perhaps, I couldn't put this feeling in to words at that time. It took some years before I could think about the meaning of prejudice or racism and to be able to articulate my thoughts on these disturbing subjects but even as a little boy I tried in my own way to make sense of the hostility that I sometimes faced in school or on the streets. When I looked in to the mirror, I saw a boy with black hair, dark brown eyes and an olive complexion looking back at me. I looked different from the children with whom I went to school. They were often blonde with blue eyes and fair skin. The difference was sometimes emphasised by other people. Sometimes children at school called me names:

"Bubble and squeak, Greek!"

There were other racist taunts or jokes; sometimes there were hostile looks or comments like,

"Go back to your own country, you bloody foreigner."

Such occurrences could happen anywhere: in the streets, on the bus, on the tube, at the shops or market place. It would leave the target of such verbal abuse feeling isolated and demeaned .There was a kind of crisis between some members of the host community and the recent arrivals from India and Pakistan or from the Caribbean and Cyprus. Some British people found it impossible to accept the immigrants who had come to live amongst them as fellow human beings and as fellow citizens. There wasn't anything that anyone could say that would change this point of view. On the street level there was verbal abuse directed at the immigrants. From a pragmatic point of view housing became a problem particularly for black people. Rooms were advertised for letting on shop notice boards but often a footnote was added on these notices indicating that " coloured people" need not apply. Employment was also very problematic for immigrants who irrespective of qualifications, skills or abilities were often given the most menial jobs. It took years before this sort of prejudice was eliminated. Indeed, a minority of English people seemed to suffer from some kind of genetic condition that prevented them from ridding themselves of the prejudice that they had towards people different from themselves.

However, the good will shown by most people in Britain far outweighed the hostility shown by a minority of racists. Anti-racist laws were passed. The Race Relations Act became law in 1965 and it was amended in subsequent years, each time giving further support to those people on the receiving end of racial prejudice. No longer could people from what became the ethnic minorities, have the rights of the ordinary citizen denied to them. Multiculturalism was introduced in schools with the aim of educating children to respect, to learn from and to enjoy each other's cultural heritage.

With political decisions that attempted to integrate the ethnic minority people into the fabric of British society, it must be said that the major political parties had introduced policies and governments had passed laws that reflected a civilised and commendable attitude towards the people who had recently arrived at these shores. This progress was indeed important but just as relevant was the attitude of the many ordinary British people who went out of their way to show that they were friendly and fair towards the new people who had come to live in Britain.

~

London and Istanbul

During the late 1950s the Cypriots in the United Kingdom were in an awkward position. In Cyprus, EOKA was conducting a guerrilla war against the British and it was, indeed, a bitter little war with casualties and high feelings on both sides. The bitterness was certainly expressed in the British policy to involve Turkey in the peace negotiations and to give her a say in the future of Cyprus. Britain, it was obvious, was determined to punish the Greek Cypriots for their rebellion against British rule.

The involvement of Turkey led to the tragic consequences of the 1974 invasion. There was rape, death and suffering. It also led to the partition of Cyprus which was the policy of Turkey from the beginning and even before her involvement in the Cyprus problem.

Despite Britain's policy towards Cyprus, it is to be noted that in the United Kingdom it self, in the streets of London where most Cypriots who had immigrated to England lived, there were hardly any hostile acts committed against Cypriots. Admittedly, there were some isolated incidents involving a fringe group of people who sometimes made racist remarks. At the time, those on the receiving end of such treatment, often felt that it was serious and a cause of insecurity and emotional suffering. And yes, indeed it was, but there was nothing official, nothing in the law of the land that showed prejudice against any group that had arrived and had established itself in the United Kingdom. Thus, most people went about their business feeling quite safe and on the whole quite secure. People worked, earned money and prospered. It might seem that the British give the impression that they are "cold" or "distant" people but at that time they exhibited an attitude towards Cypriots that was on the whole, apart from isolated incidents, civilised and hospitable despite the fact that in Cyprus the EOKA were engaged in conflict against British forces.

This attitude was in stark contrast to that of the Turkish Government, when in 1955 the news reached Constantinople that the Greeks of Cyprus were demanding Enosis with Greece; they orchestrated a pogrom against the Greek minority of Constantinople. Turkish nationalist fanatics encouraged by the Turkish Government attacked the homes and property of the Greek community. The mob, in a wild rampage burnt, looted and killed indiscriminately the Greeks who they could lay their hands on while the Turkish police and troops stood idly by and turned a blind eye. This was the final act that led almost to all of the remaining Greeks of Constantinople to seek a safer and more secure place in which to live. Over 100,000 people of Greek origin then made the journey to Greece, leaving behind their wealth and their properties. This was a community that had been wealthy and established. They were forced to abandon all their possessions. They were robbed. They were humiliated. They were driven out of the city that their ancestors had founded and in most cases they arrived in Greece as penniless refugees.*

The contrast between the British attitude and the attitude of the Turkish Government to the same problem could not be greater. The one shines as a civilised example and the other is an expression of an extreme fanatical nationalism.

The authorities in the United Kingdom took all precautions, as far as it was possible, to ensure the safety and security of all people and not for one moment was it ever considered to allow the racist thugs a freehand in what they intended to do. The individual unpleasantness, expressed in a casual manner by someone passing by, a word or a hostile look cannot be compared with wholesale murder, rape, robbery and expulsion of an entire group of people because of political events that were, in any case, totally beyond their control.

*The Istanbul Pogrom, 6-7, September, 1955. Greeks call this dreadful episode "The Septemvriana". It refers to the events that were organised by the Turkish Army's Tactical Mobilization Force. The events were set in motion by the news that the Turkish Consulate in Thesaloniki that was also the house in which, Kemal Attaturk, the founder of modern Turkey had been born in, had suffered damage in a bomb attack. The person responsible was a Turkish security guard who had been arrested and had confessed his crime. The Turkish media, however, reported the bombing of the consulate but had deliberately omitted the part played by the Turkish security guard and entirely blamed the event on the Greeks. This deliberate disinformation led to the well planned and orchestrated riots in which the Greek community of Istanbul was savagely attacked by a frenzied Turkish mob.

Speaking and Listening

Even as a young man, I had realised that living in London was an enriching, worthwhile and positive experience. Though as a child I had stood feeling alone and isolated in that classroom where I had been hit by my teacher or was taunted by a passerby in a busy street in North London, these experiences did not embitter me nor were they really important. To counteract these isolated events, I had innumerable constructive and sometimes brilliant experiences in school. My teachers were mostly very kind, helpful and caring and it is these people that I thank for not allowing the seeds of disillusion to grow or to flourish in my mind. School for me had been mostly a place of interest, creativity and where I was able to achieve my potential. I certainly very quickly picked up the ability to communicate in English. In my first year of school in Cyprus, I was taught to read phonically and soon after when we had arrived in England, I used those skills to decipher the English alphabet and to embark on my interest in reading that has delighted me throughout my life. My love of reading stories I know, harked back to the folk tales my grandmother narrated to my sister and me some years before, in our village in Cyprus. Folk tales are the same the world over and this was a strong link between my past in Cyprus and my boyhood experiences in England. The more English I learnt the more I grew in confidence.

My sister had learnt English fairly quickly, but she was not as fluent as me. At fifteen she left school and started working in the same factory as my mother. In fact she often complained that it was unfair that she was not given the opportunity to study and to reach her potential. What happened to her also happened to thousands of other Cypriot young women. The Cypriots, who came to England in the 1950s and early 60s, came with the attitude that the role of a young woman is to marry, bear children and to be of help to her husband. Many felt that there wasn't any need to educate a girl, for there would not be any use for this education. This was a crude, naive and very narrow minded attitude. In time, for the Cypriot community, this attitude changed but it did not change soon enough to benefit my sister Kika. She worked with mother; she was a teenage bride, bore children before she was even twenty years of age and then worked very hard to raise them. She was trapped by a blind tradition.

Our parents, who were loving and kind, were also trapped in their perception of what was right for their daughter and even now, in England, there are other ethnic communities who continue to perceive their young women as objects that are owned and who must obey customs and traditions from far way. When these young women sometimes dare to refute the unwritten laws of their communities, they become outcasts and sometimes even worse. My experience was in sharp contrast to that of my sister. Sadly, we were not treated as being of equal importance. Boys were elevated while girls were subjugated.

Having learnt to speak English quite fluently and in addition having acquired the ability to read and write with some accuracy, my importance in the family grew substantially for an eleven year old boy. My father never learnt English beyond a few spoken phrases. I was soon to become his interpreter and translator. This included the reading and response to official letters relating to tax, social benefits, housing and other such issues. I was given the responsibility for writing letters or completing important forms. I always accompanied my father to the Labour Exchange on occasions when he was seeking employment or sorting out issues of tax or benefits. Mother also used me as an interpreter usually at the doctors or for her hospital appointments. I remember how after mother's examination, the friendly GP looked at me with an admiring smile, offered me a sweet and said,

"You're doing a fine job, Master Loizou, a really fine job. Well done!"

Of no less importance to my language development was when father on a regular basis asked me to interpret the BBC news as it was being presented on the television. I do not know whether father had an interest in the news or whether it was because he felt that this exercise was helping me acquire important language skills, but it became our habit that when ever possible we would settle down together in front of the television and I then attempted to perform an instant translation of the news. This was one of the few father and son activities that he and I engaged in. I am quite certain that having only recently acquired a fairly fluent ability in spoken English, the accuracy of my translations might have been found wanting. My father would sit comfortably on his arm chair and sometimes smiled in a knowing amused manner. It was probably at the wild inaccuracies and exaggerations of my translations. There was never any criticism of my abilities and I am certain that indeed this exercise was intended by my father to help me with both my Greek and English. My fluency in both these languages gave me a respect in the family that had come to rely on my language skills to make sense of British Society. Not only did they call upon me to interpret the language but also to explain what politicians were saying on television or the action and dialogue of films and even the jokes in comedy shows on television. Our favourite comedians were Charlie Drake and Norman Wisdom whose humour was easy to follow for my parents because much of it was based on farce. We laughed heartily at Charlie Drake stumbling off ladders into pots or buckets full of water or at Norman Wisdom in his cloth cap, creating a crisis for Mr Grimsdale at every turn. We sat around the television on Saturday nights enjoying films and shows like many other ordinary families. This was in a sense an initiation into British culture and we were unknowingly very keen receptors. My parents were forever trying to work out what was going on, what was being said.

"Tell me what he is saying, Fotaki. What are they going to do? What is going to happen?" they asked me every five minutes.

Sometimes my sister and I really protested because we found the constant interruptions from our parents prevented us from enjoying the programmes. This didn't stop them from persisting!

I had a sense even then that my parents were deeply interested in this new place that they had come to, that they were curious and inquisitive to know about its nature and spirit but recognised that language was a difficult obstacle, a barrier which prevented most people like them who had had very little formal education from finding a true understanding of British society. So I became their ears and their tongue, helping them in their challenging new life in the great metropolis of London.

In addition to this, my visits to the Labour Exchange with my father where I interpreted questions about work skills, previous employments or benefits for unemployment gave me a sense of adult concerns about work and the importance of earnings.

One day when we were sitting quietly at home in response to my questions about why we were yet again going to the Labour Exchange, my father tried to explain the importance of this organisation for working people. He settled back into his chair as if he had a lot to speak about and that it would take some time to do so. He spoke in a simple and direct manner as if he was speaking with an adult who could comprehend the subject of the conversation:

"Fotaki", he spoke with warmth and affection.

"We have come from a beautiful homeland. Cyprus is a place that has been blessed by God with many gifts. It has mountains covered with forests, it has a rich soil so that crops grow in abundance..."

"So why did we leave Cyprus and come to England, Father?"

"I was about to explain. You see, the land and the wealth always seemed to belong to the very rich people who were never happy to share and who always wanted more and more wealth. People like us had next to nothing. We could only sell our labour. We had to work incredibly hard and receive very little in return. Sometimes I worked as a labourer, a hamali, loading and unloading cargo ships in Famagusta Port or I mixed cement and carried bricks on a building site, burning in the heat of the summer sun and not having enough money at the end of the week for our basic needs. Sometimes there was not enough food in the house and your mother and I went without food so you and your sister could have some thing and not go to bed feeling hungry."

I looked at him and wondered whether grandmother had judged him harshly when she often called him a waster and that mother would always be unhappy with such a husband. However, I still remained uncertain about what all this had to do with the Labour Exchange. I remained silent and attentive. He continued:

"The problem was that working people in Cyprus had almost no rights. If you were unskilled you could be laid off a job and then there would be no money for the family. This happened to me many times. Perhaps for a while I managed to find work building a villa for some rich man. After a few months when the job was completed the contractor dismissed us until he had another project but this might take months."

He sometimes paused as if to reflect on the details of what he was saying and then when he was satisfied he resumed his explanation.

"In England the working people are better organised. If you don't have a job the Labour Exchange will help you to find one and if you have no money they will help you until you can earn some for yourself. That is why we go to the Labour Exchange. It is to find work so that we can live. One day, Fotaki, when you are an adult and have a family you will realise that to have a job is the most important thing in your life. A man without employment is not a man. How can you live not knowing whether you can feed your children? How many times can you go to your relatives who might not have very much themselves and ask them for money and how many times can you ask the grocer for credit? You begin to feel ashamed and useless. The Labour Exchange helps me to find work and that is why I came to England. I am here to work."

He looked at me expecting me to understand the plight of the working man in Cyprus and in comparison the practical advantages that working people had in England.

The other activity that brought us together was when I translated the BBC evening news and this activity also had a long term impact upon me. Through this process I became intensely interested in current affairs. I wanted to know what was going on in England and in the world. I followed news stories from Parliament and began to understand that there were two main political parties, the Labour Party and the Conservative Party and they were always at loggerheads with each other. In the conversations that I had with my father and which usually occurred after the early evening news, he explained their difference in a simple and lucid manner:

"Fotaki," he addressed me affectionately.

"The Labour Party is for the ordinary working people like us. They want to give us better conditions at work. They want to have a better health service and build new schools for the children. The Conservatives are for the rich people who want even more then what they have already, just like the rich people in Cyprus who build fine villas and drive expensive cars imported from England and who don't give a damn if the ordinary people around them are going hungry."

He felt that Harold Wilson was a politician who could be relied upon to help ordinary working people. Father always voted for Labour and he was overjoyed when in 1967 Harold Wilson made his famous visit to Moscow.

"He is not like the Conservative politicians. The people can trust Wilson because he is always trying to help the workers. He is friends with Russia because he is also socialist. He is the leader of the Labour Party who will always try to help working people and they don't care if you are black, white or Cypriot."

Thus I began to think about party politics from quite an early age. Another great influence was "The Times" newspaper with its division of the news into "Home News", "European News" and "World News" categories. I began to follow with increasing clarity and understanding the threads in stories that held together the changing circumstances and changing fortunes of countries and political personalities - The Kennedys, Fidel Castro, The Bay of Pigs, The Cuba Missile Crises, The Six Day War, Vietnam, Cyprus - an endless list of events and stories presented in the newspapers like the never ending stories of Shaharazade or the soap operas that fascinate modern television audiences. This interest in current affairs that grabbed my attention at such a young age became a compulsion that I still experience. A daily read of at least one serious newspaper is a must for me and if time allows a further reading of international news from the internet. Little did my father realise that when he requested me to translate the BBC evening news on television, that one day this habit would turn me into an insatiable consumer of the news.

The Duveen Gallery

As a sixteen year old boy I began to understand and appreciate the English teenage culture around me and in particular the unique cultural advantages of living in the capital city of England. The British Museum must count as one of those huge advantages. How could any one with an interest in history and culture not be impressed with the epic treasures contained within its wide halls?

On my first visit, I stood by the tall iron gates of the museum and looked upon the imposing facade of Ionic columns. This was a Greek temple built in the classical style. It seemed as if some holy shrine dedicated to Zeus had been magically transplanted from the vale of Arcadia and brought to these northern shores to house treasures from the four corners of the earth. From every point of view, I felt that this was a very special place, even though I did not exactly know what I expected to find inside the museum. However, I was not going to be disappointed.

With dozens of other visitors I walked along the broad paved pathway leading to the stone steps. As I approached the portico, I gazed up in wonder at the massive fluted columns that supported the pediment and the frieze with its fine sculptures depicting the ancient gods of Olympus. For the first time but not the last, I entered through the massive doors of this incredible temple dedicated to the history and achievements of mankind not realising that this would be the beginning of a long and loving relationship that I would have with this very special institution.

The first area of interest that I wondered into was the hall containing the Egyptian collection. There were mummies of men and women, of boys and girls, there were even mummies of cats and dogs. The gallery displayed a huge number of statues in stiff postures gazing blankly into space. Then there was the Rosetta Stone, a slab of black granite with Egyptian hieroglyphics, Assyrian cuneiform and Greek letters neatly carved upon it. The three texts carved on the stone corresponded in meaning with each other. This was of great interest to me because we had studied at school about the importance of the Rosetta Stone and how it had enabled Jean-Francois Champillion and Thomas Young, two brilliant 19th century scholars, to decipher the as yet unknown ancient languages of Egypt and Assyria by comparing it with the familiar ancient Greek. As I stood there, I tried to use my knowledge of Greek to read something from the stone but to no avail for it all seemed strange and uncommon; I could not make any sense of it and so I moved on, strolling through the wide halls crammed to the brim with treasures from other lands.

How could it be, I asked myself, that so many artefacts could have been brought from the four corners of the earth to reside in the heart of London? The answer to this question was at that particular moment in time uncertain and unclear to me. I also experienced, even from my earliest visits that despite the magnificence of the British Museum, Egyptian mummies, statues and indeed the other display pieces were somehow in an alien environment, far from home, out of context.

I continued to stroll through the halls of the museum and went from the Egyptian gallery to the halls that contained the collection from Greece. The stiff and lifeless style of Egyptian sculpture gave way to lifelike and idealised human forms of classical or Hellenistic art.

At the entrance of a great hall I noticed the bust of Perikles the Athenian. The bust was familiar to me from pictures in history books. This famous sculpted portrait of white marble with the name of Perikles Xanthippou boldly carved at the base, depicted the famous statesman as having fine, noble features, with a full curly beard and wearing the helmet of an Athenian hoplite. I could not fail to notice that most visitors barely glanced at it as they entered the main hall of Greek exhibits but I was drawn to it because I knew this sculpture from pictures in history books and I knew the name of the man it portrayed. I was familiar with the knowledge that this man was one of the great personalities of ancient Greece.

I stood before the bust of Perikles and gazed upon his countenance with the feeling that this was the image of a very special man and a hero. This was indeed strange that I should have had such an emotional response to the image of Periklis because at the time I had only an inkling of his achievements. I knew that it was he who commissioned the building of the Parthenon and the unique sculptures that were going to adorn it. Later I discovered that Periklis worked very hard to make Athens the most important city state in Greece and he would have achieved much more had he not suffered an untimely death during a fateful plague that had struck the city during the early stages of the Peloponnisian War that would eventually prove to be disastrous for Athens. If the noble Periklis who had achieved so much for his city could speak to us, the Greeks of today, what would he say? I am certain that he would admonish us over many issues and perhaps like a school master complain that we have not achieved the great potential that was expected of us but most of all he would have been truly horrified that so many art treasures from Greece had been looted and stolen, including so many of the sculptures that he himself as the leading statesman of Athens had commissioned and that these were now in the possession of other people. Perhaps he would have uttered the following reprimands:

"How, dear fellow Greeks, could it have been possible for you to fall from the glorious heights achieved by us, you ancestors, to the dismal circumstances that you find yourselves in today? The sons of slaves have achieved much more then you whose fathers fought and were victorious at Salamis and Marathon, who saved all of Europe from the oppression of the cruel Persian Empire. You have allowed the sacred Greek soil to be trampled upon by the foot of the barbarian and our heritage to be stolen from us..."

If by some strange phenomenon Periklis was to utter these words to us, what feeble excuses could we give him? How could we explain to the great statesman the confusion and failings of the modern Greek state. Imagine the disappointment that he would feel. I gradually moved on from the marble image of Periklis into what, I discovered to be the Duveen Gallery that had been purpose built to house the marble statues of the Parthenon.

As a sixteen year old boy I understood very little about the great achievement that these works of art represented but even so, when I looked at the statue of the reclining god, or at the figures of the Lapiths and Centaurs or the formation of cavalry riding on I was awestruck by the beauty, the natural appearance and the feeling of movement forever captured in those stones. The sculptured youthful riders forever young, riding on in their cavalry formation, the Lapiths and centaurs forever locked in a never ending battle oblivious to the passing of time while from one generation to the next people look on in wonder and admiration.

I left the museum on that day feeling that I had made a great discovery. Here was the primary evidence that would feed my passion for ancient Greek history. The marbles were inspiring and wonderful to behold. They had stimulated my love for classical history and that has remained with me. These sculptures gave me pride in my Greek heritage and I can say without hesitation that the first time I saw the Parthenon marbles has remained an unforgettable experience.

Many years after, when I had the opportunity to visit the Acropolis of Athens, I found myself standing with a group of tourists from England, listening to the tourist guide who was describing to us the architectural and artistic merits of the Parthenon. Perhaps I was the only person amongst the group who noticed the change in her voice; perhaps I might have even imagined it but I felt as I continued to listen to her description of the ancient temple, that her voice had taken on a poetic quality proclaiming to us, her listeners and to the world beyond, that here on the Acropolis, in the shadow of Athena's temple was and continues to be the beating heart of Greece. Her final words referred to the Parthenon marbles and what she said epitomised what every Greek person feels. I clearly remember her words that were full of emotion as she spoke:

"The Parthenon marbles" she said, "are unlike any other treasure produced by our ancient forefathers. The very soul of what is best about Greek civilization is in the fibre of the marbles. While these holy stones are held captive in a far off land, Greece itself remains a captive..."

Her words had touched my heart and I could not but shed some tears there on the holy hill of Athens and to feel more strongly then ever that the Parthenon marbles should be immediately returned to their rightful owners, the people of Greece.

It is worth to briefly note how the Parthenon marbles came to be in England rather then in their country of origin:

~

The marbles in the Duveen Gallery of the British Museum were an integral part of the Parthenon and the Acropolis of Athens until Thomas Elgin otherwise known by his title Lord Elgin removed numerous pieces of sculpture from the temple. Some of the pieces were crudely cut away from the building without consideration for the damage that this action caused. This was undoubtedly an act of vandalism that cannot be defended.

Greece at the time was in the last few years of Ottoman occupation and Elgin who was British Ambassador at Constantinople had obtained a "firman" or "Permit" from the Sultan. This document has been used as an argument for the legality of Elgin's act of vandalism. The Greeks, however, have argued that the legality of the "firman" is in question and that Elgin had committed an act of theft but that at the time they were powerless to prevent it.

Since that time, Greek governments have frequently requested that the Parthenon marbles should be returned but the British Government which had purchased the marbles from Lord Elgin in 1816 refused to return these statues to their place of origin. It does not surprise me that there has been a very strong support amongst intellectuals in United Kingdom for the return of the marbles. Intelligent people always have a sensitive understanding of what is right and what is just. This was very early on given a voice by the poet and Philhellene Lord Byron who in his verses from "Child Harold" comments on this subject:

> Dull is the eye that weeps not to see
> Thy walls defaced, thy mouldering shrines removed
> By British hands, which it had best behoved
> To guard those relics ne'er to be restored.
> Cursed be the hour when from their isle they roved,
> And once again thy hapless bosom gored,
> And snatche'd thy shrinking gods to northern climes abhored!

~

As a school boy and even later as a student teacher I regularly visited the British Museum, enjoying its unique treasures. Ignorantly, I had not really thought much about the debate concerning the return of the marbles. How I became more interested and then supported the idea of the return happened inadvertently: It was when I visited the church of the Apostle Andreas in Kentish Town. I had gone there to arrange for the Baptism of my little daughter Louisa. The Bishop who seemed an enigmatic personality had a copy of "The Times" and following his discovery that I was a teacher, he seemed eager to engage in conversation regarding a particular article that referred to the return of the marbles to Greece.

"What do you think about this issue? Should not the British return the marbles?"

It was the first time I was presented with this question. Of course I had respect for the Bishop and I did not want to appear ignorant about such a subject. I managed on the spur of the moment to stammer an answer.

" I think they are unique sculptures...I have seen them several times in the British Museum....and the British really do look after them and value them from a scholarly point of view......but they are ours......they do belong to Greece, they are a part of Greek Heritage.......they should be returned."

I felt fairly satisfied with the answer that I gave to his unexpected question. He seemed pleased with my response and from that moment I began to take an almost compulsive interest in the debate. I read every article in the newspapers related to this subject and more recently I have been looking at documents on the internet. Now more then any other time, I really do feel, that with the inauguration of a world class museum in Athens which has been acclaimed as an architectural master piece, the marbles must be returned to their place of origin.

However, the debate goes on without much hope that the Greek people will successfully retrieve their stolen national treasures at any point in the near future.

Mrs Evens and Mr Ward

By the time I had reached secondary school I was very fluent and articulate in English. I could speak, read and write English as well as any English boy of my age. This enabled me to compete successfully in every aspect of school life. School had always remained an exciting place for me. I was encouraged by my mother, who, despite the fact that she could hardly speak English and had a full time job to contend with, turned up at parents' evenings to find out about my progress. I would be at her side, interpreting her questions into English and my teachers' comments into Greek. Sometimes my teachers joked with me,

"Are you sure, you are telling your mum what I am saying?"

I looked at them and smiled, knowing that I was only being teased. I loved school and I was a very hard working student. The old habit of listening to stories first from my grandmother in Cyprus and later when I'd learned to read stories from books widely available to me from the school library sharpened my appetite for English. My reading at school had already evolved and developed into a serious passion. I sensed my love for novels and poems even as a thirteen or fourteen year old. I was very fortunate that I had teachers who inspired me. One such teacher was Mrs Evens. She was a Welsh lady who seemed very old, grand and even aristocratic. She dressed in the finery of the Edwardian era and appeared in every sense impressive to those around her. Her warmth was like a powerful magnet drawing us to her, enabling her to guide us through the reading of "Pygmalion" by George Bernard Shaw or "Macbeth" by William Shakespeare. Her sensitive interpretations, her ability to make us understand the stories, the themes and the language of literature were important moments in my growing love for books. How amusing I had found her reading of Eliza Doolittle and how thought inspiring were her lessons on accent and class! Mrs Evens was always full of praise for my reading and writing. She often displayed my work on the classroom display board. For both my first and second year at school she awarded me the prize for the most progress in English. For both the forth and fifth years I was awarded the English prize for being top of the class in that subject.

Mr Ward was the Head of English at Highbury Grove School at the time when I was studying there for my "A" level GCEs. He had an imposing Hollywood appearance; something like Charlton Heston, with a tanned complexion, steel grey, curly hair and a voice that became melodious when he spoke about a favourite poem or a play. He was a Cambridge graduate, a master of his subject. We, his students, knew that he could recite from texts and the beauty of his recital from the opening lines of "Paradise Lost" or from "The Canterbury Tales" were to me the most wonderful moments that, as a boy, I experienced in the classroom. He was able to make his lessons not only enjoyable but also inspirational. It seemed to be important to him that at least some of his students should specialise in English at university and therefore towards the end of our "A" level course he sometimes commented that we should be seriously thinking of following a degree course in the "Queen of Subjects" which for him, of course, was the study of English Literature.

Mrs Evans and Mr Ward were magnificent teachers who passed on to me and other students their love of literature. It's true what they say, that a person never forgets a good teacher.

In class, I read whatever I could get my hands on. Greek myths and legends were amongst my favourites. Odysseus resurfaced, blinding Polyphemos and escaping from the cave. This legend from Homer's 'The Odyssey' stayed with me and seemed to symbolise the struggle of the immigrant child trying to make sense of his new world, or the adult who faced challenging circumstances. At secondary school I studied 'The Odyssey' for my GCE in Greek Literature. Later I re-read chapters from 'The Odyssey' while studying 'Ulysses' by James Joyce at University. The story continued to re-appear at different points in my life and what is Homer's tale if not of a character who, through fate and fortune, finds himself far from home and who is away for so long that home has inevitably changed beyond all recognition but whose memory, nevertheless, still pricks his heart with nostalgia. Home became a distant romantic dream, a yearning that was not related to our everyday new found life. Recently, quite by accident, I came across a poem entitled "Ithaka" by CP Cavafy. The poem delighted me and had a profound effect. This is the poem in translation:

> As you begin your journey to Ithaka
> hope your way is a long ,
> full of adventure, full of discovery.
> Laistrygonians, Cyclops,
> vengeful Poseidon – don't be afraid of them:
> you'll never find things like that on your way
> as long as you keep your courage raised high,
> as long as a rare excitement

effects your soul and your body.
Laistrygonians, Cyclopes,
wild Poseidon you won't encounter them
unless you bring them with you in your soul,
unless your soul erects them in front of you.

Hope your path is a long one.
May there be many summer mornings when,
With pleasure and oh what joy,
you enter unfamiliar harbours for the first time;
may you stop at Phoenician trading stations
to buy delicate things,
mother of pearl and coral, amber and ebony,
sensual perfume of many a kind –
as many sensual perfumes as you can;
and may you visit numerous Egyptian cities
to learn and go on learning from their wise men.

Keep Ithaka always in your thoughts.
Arriving there is your destiny.
But don't rush the journey.
Better if it endures for years,
so you're aged by the time you arrive to your old home,
wealthy with all you've earned on the way,
not expecting Ithaka to make you wealthy.

This poem made me feel that we all journey from Ithaka. We all have dangerous encounters with Laistrygonians or Cyclopes. We mostly overcome them and continue our quest for Ithaka. But Ithaka is not a geographical place that you can return to. Laistrygonians can be racist teachers who role up your sleeve and smack your hand until it painfully stings and Cyclopes can be nasty old men who might spit out some racist venom at you in the street. The poem is about present threats and challenges that the individual might be faced with and how the individual must conquer these fearful, negative forces and calmly journey to his or her destination where ever that may be. It is the spiritual fulfilment and understanding that the earth is the earth whether you are in Cyprus, England or Ithaka.

I read through the poems of the bilingual text. I read the poems in Greek and often referred to the English translation to make sense of some of the words that I could not understand in Greek. On reflection the bilingual text represents me and others like me from a different culture and ethnicity who came here or were born here in England and who are both British and something else. This something else, developed and used correctly can only enrich the tapestry of British cultural life, making it colourful and complex.

"Rupert the Bear", "Peter Rabbit", "The Beano", "The Beazer" and "The Valiant" were the springboards of my reading. By the time I was Twelve, I was fluent in reading in English. Suddenly I could read comics and books, newspapers and magazines. I was able to find out about the present and about the past. Inevitably this led me to read and research about the sad history of the oppressed people of Cyprus and their desire for freedom and peace.

~

The Republic of Cyprus was born in 1960. The complexity of the constitution, the demons of nationalism from Greece and Turkey, the intrigues of the British foreign office in its endeavours to maintain British interests in the area meant that the newly born baby would find it very tricky to survive in the future. There was open conflict in 1963 and in 1964. Greek Cypriots and Turkish Cypriots were at each others throats. Without realising it, they were the puppets in a much bigger show in which foreign interests were put above the interests of Cyprus and the Cypriots. There were both internal and external threats to Cyprus. The Turkish Cypriots had been convinced that it was in their interest to seek partition and the Greek Cypriots through political misjudgement, to seek Enosis with Greece. Turkey could not accept the idea of a predominantly Greek island united with Greece near its underbelly. Greece wanted to be bigger and stronger. It seems that despite the catastrophe of Asia Minor in 1922, "The Big Idea" had not yet died entirely. It should have been buried and not resurrected to cause untold misery to the people of Cyprus. Britain saw the conflict as an opportunity. While the differences and divisions on the island cemented themselves into a new political reality, Britain re-entered the scene as the peace maker. The former colonial master now presented himself as the preserver of the peace in a country that had now proved too chaotic to rule itself. For Britain, a weak and divided Cyprus meant that its control of Episcopi and Akrotiri bases could not be challenged. Further, Britain exploited the ensuing political chaos by refusing to pay the Republic of Cyprus the agreed amount of "rent" for the base areas. The weak and anaemic Republic of Cyprus could not challenge in real terms the withdrawal of payment by the British Government. Unfortunately, for Cyprus much worse was to follow.

~

The unfolding and developing Cyprus problem led me to devour the newspaper in search of articles about Cyprus. I felt like a Cypriot who was cut off from playing my part in the unfolding story of Cyprus but in fact, I was only a London school boy with an emerging sense of Britishness.

At school, Greek Cypriot boys and girls entered into discussion with each other and with Turkish Cypriot students. From hindsight it is easy to see how naive we all were in our entrenched nationalistic beliefs. Instead of being taught that we had common interests we were divided by the hate of outdated nationalisms and interpretations of history that did not strictly apply to Cyprus and its people. But despite the bitterness and hate between Greek and Turkish Cypriots on the island and despite our heated discussions about inter communal politics of Cyprus, in London we continued to enjoy friendships and warm neighbourly relationships. Was this not a clear indication that the divisions in Cyprus were artificially created and if given the opportunity, without outside interference, would the two communities in Cyprus not be able to overcome all their problems?

~

"The Times" and "The Guardian became favourite newspapers because they contained so much serious reporting of British and foreign news. By the time I had entered the sixth form at Highbury Grove School, I was quite addicted to the reading of broadsheets and showed a critical awareness and response to much that was presented in them. Parallel to this, I was by now reading from the canon of English Literature "Pygmalion" by George Bernard Shaw, "Macbeth", "Othello", "The Tempest", "A Midsummer Nights Dream" by

William Shakespeare, "1984", "Brave New World" "The Portrait of the Artist" and so on. The impact on me was enormous. These are only some of the books that have changed my life because they taught me to think not only from a literary point of view but to also consider ethics and morality, justice and injustice, right and wrong. They helped me to give form and shape to my values as a person. In addition, having some brilliant teachers of English like the silver haired, smiling, talented Mr Ward who could recite chunks from Shakespeare or Chaucer and bring to life the texts, or the enthusiastic kind, generous and caring Mrs Evans who would contextualise and put everything into perspective, passed on their love of the subject, and though by now I am certain that they are no longer with us for they were old when I was no more than a teenager, their love for literature also certainly lives in me and in other former students who had passed through their classrooms.

How does one repay such people, who pass that which is good and worthwhile in life to the younger generation so that goodness spreads out benevolently from one person to the next? It is with their prompting and encouragement that I began to understand the importance of passing my exams and gaining a place at university. They encouraged me with their words and gestures, their kind feelings and their belief that I could achieve my goals.

When once, in conversation with Mr Ward, I informed him that I wanted to become a teacher of English, he beamed with a smile and graciously commented,

"The profession needs good teachers and, Fotis, if my hunch is right, you will be a very good teacher."

At these kind words from a teacher who I sincerely respected and deeply admired, I felt at the same time both pride and humility. For my part I tried to do my best not only for my own benefit but also because I would have felt a terrible embarrassment to have failed the people who had put such faith in me. Mr Ward's kind and caring attitude, his ability to motivate and teach us his students and to make us believe that we could succeed when we sometimes felt that we were on mission impossible inspired me as a student and continues to inspire me even today in my work as a teacher.

The Young.....and the Old

As a teenager, I sensed the excitement of being in London. It was my home, the place where I lived, went to school, where my friends lived and where I, as a fifteen or sixteen year old, began to explore some of the life that it could offer a young man. The excitement of this city has never ceased to amaze me but even more so when one spring morning I decided to travel by tube from Finsbury Park, where we lived, to Leicester Square. I'd heard my friends talking about the West End and I had been very rarely with my parents to see it. They sometimes spoke about going to the "pigeons" by which they meant Trafalgar Square or the Queen's Palace by which they meant Buckingham Palace.

This was a time when I had begun to dress fashionably and to have a trendy teenage appearance. I wore flare jeans and grown my hair in the style of the Rolling Stones. And one day, feeling rather "with it", I decided to catch the tube and head for the West End. On this occasion and countless other times, with my school friends, we walked along Oxford Street gazing in to the shop windows. There were thousands of people crowding the pavements. Loud music could be heard from shops, bistros and restaurants. There was the general feeling that this was the beginning of something new and exiting in fashion, music, dance and in the attitude of people to past conventions. The young felt that "the times they are a changing" and as previous younger generations, we felt that the exciting new future belonged to us. It was without a doubt, the beginning of new kind of cultural revolution that was expressed significantly in the popular music of the period by Bob Dylan, The Beatles, Hendrix and others.

There was also a powerful representation of the times in the art of Andy Warhole and Roy Lichtenstein who captured and expressed the mood of that time in their paintings. Certainly, for those of us who were in our teens there seemed to be so much going on to inspire our imaginations. We were dazzled by the "happenings" that brought together psychedelic music, film projection and dance all going on at the same time. I began to collect music albums by various artists. My hair was long; I wore yellow tinted glasses in the style of John Lennon and tried to dress in keeping with the psychedelic style. In fact, it was a great time in my life when I'd also completed my "A" level GCEs and was planning on going to university. While all this was going on, I'd hardly noticed that the smoking of cannabis was becoming more and more popular, particularly at the "happenings." LSD also reared its ugly head and was associated closely with the psychedelic movement. People at that time just did not realise that the use of illicit drugs by the very few, who probably had little idea of what they were doing, would eventually lead to the drug taking epidemic that has developed since that time. From hindsight, it is easy to see how terribly naive we all were but I suppose that is true of every generation who in the course of time looks back at its experiences.

I continued to be fascinated by what was going on, particularly in London. I was like a sponge absorbing the excitement of that time. I bought my first record and my taste in music began to develop. I dressed like other teenagers, enjoyed the discos and the parties.

Alongside this cultural development, I took my studies seriously. I aspired to get a place at university. My teachers were friendly and encouraging. I went on school visits to the theatre and saw my first Shakespeare performance at the Old Vic. It was a memorable production of "The Tempest" in which Prospero and his daughter Miranda are exiled from their home and find themselves in difficult circumstances on an island on which they have to make a new life. I had also begun to appreciate serious films. My cultural life was undergoing a sea change and what is most of all surprising is how I felt completely natural at the transformation. At no point did I feel that I was discovering a foreign culture or that I did not belong to this environment. I felt completely that London is where I belonged and that it was absolutely natural for me to enjoy the music of the Beatles, the sound of the Rolling Stones, the lyrics of Bob Dylan, to read the plays of Shakespeare or the poetry of William Wordsworth but at the same time also felt very natural and normal with my Greek Cypriot home life. It seems that our sense of Britishness had started to emerge in a distinct form. There was no conscious recognition of this; the change was gradual, in fact, it had started almost from the moment we set foot in the United kingdom but now it could be identified more distinctly in the bilingualism and the biculturalism of the young Cypriots who had grown up in London.

At home we continued to speak Greek because my parents never really learnt English well enough to be able to communicate with it in an uninhibited way. We ate traditional Cypriot food which was, of course, delicious. All our friends and visitors to our home were other Cypriots. We visited their homes and we spoke about Cyprus or about who was getting married to whom within our community. The high point of the week was Sunday. There was always some thing happening. Often there was a wedding party or we would have an invitation for dinner, usually from friends who hailed from our village in Cyprus or from some relative who had made the journey to

England. Sometimes there would be guests at our house where mother and father welcomed them with traditional Cypriot hospitality. Whatever the occasion, dinner was always a feast. There was koubebeia or what some people call dolmades, rice mixed with mince meat, sprinkled with herbs wrapped in vine leaves like little parcels and cooked in a watery tomato sauce. My favourite dish was kolokassi yiahni, a sweet potato cooked with chicken in a tomato sauce, sprinkled with fresh lemon. With the delicious dinner there was usually a bottle of Johnny Walker, Red Label. Seated around the table, eating and drinking the talk would ensue. The topics were usually predictable: whose son or daughter was getting engaged or married, the birth of children and the latest developments in the never ending saga of the Cyprus problem. As a boy I would sit and listen to the conversation of the adults. I observed their habits and internalised their wonderful way of speaking in the Greek Cypriot dialect. I felt even then that I belonged to two worlds and that I could easily slip from the one into the other. My parent's world still remained that of their village in Cyprus. Yes, they were now in London but their only sense of London was their journey to work and back. The only time that they made some kind of contact with English people was when they caught the bus or went to the market. This is when they had the opportunity to use the very little English that they had managed to acquire. "One shilling, Kentish Town, please" or "Six pence, Angel, please." They knew how to ask for their correct fair on the bus simply because it was vital to be able to get around. Another activity that was also important and had to be managed in English was buying food. "One pound apples, please" or "Two pound tomatoes, please". The language was straight forward but it was enough for their simple needs. Sadly, like my parents, most of the ordinary Cypriots who were brave enough to make the journey to what was a distant land for a better life hardly moved beyond that basic level of communicating in English. For them, the most meaningful and satisfying experience was within their own community and within their homes. They spoke their own language and held on to their values and way of life. No real change ever occurred to them. The influence of the new land that they had come to was very marginal and this did not change with time. They remained socially and psychologically in their village. The only change was geography. They actually lived in London. They were like plants that could not take root in new soil; they could not flourish and develop but they did survive and very significantly made it possible for the young to move forward, to grow roots and to flourish in the new landscape.

The Old Dialect and the New Language

It is inevitable that time, experience and geography are catalyst for change. It may be that for my parents and their generation who had made the decision to leave their home land and to make a new life in England, ironically for them who had dared to undertake such an adventure, change remained minimal. They came from a society that was highly traditional and conservative. They felt no need to change and apart from that the new society into which they had arrived had strong social boundaries that made it difficult to join. So they became a community within a community, living and co existing side by side amongst millions of English people. At that time, perhaps this co-existence was enough for it was a time when Cypriots and other immigrants to England were settling down and finding their way in a complex North European industrial society.

For those of us who arrived in England as babies or young children and for those who in due course were born here, it was never going to be sufficient to be a member of a community within a community. England with its rich language, culture and way of life was irresistibly waiting to absorb the newcomers as it had done to newcomers in the past. So we would go to church, to Greek weekend schools, mix socially with other Cypriots and to all intents and purposes gave respect to our parents' aspirations for us. We attended English state schools, became increasingly fluent in spoken English to the point where in due course English became our main language rather then Greek but we still continued to speak Greek in the Cypriot dialect.

This gave us a sense of identity and reminded us of our homeland. We felt that if we were to suddenly return to Cyprus we would fit in without any problems and that our language would be just like everybody else. But many people in Cyprus felt that Cypriots should be closer to Greece and this also meant speaking like our brothers on the mainland. I was as yet unaware of this new and as it later became false attitude to how Cypriots were meant to speak. Up to that moment in time I was quite happy and comfortable speaking in my heavy Cypriot dialect that I had learnt in Sotira and Stylloi as a little child and also because I knew no other way of speaking Greek. I was comfortable and relaxed about how I spoke, that is until we were visited by a friend from Cyprus. Our visitor was a young man named Bambos Kitsis who regarded himself as a person with modern ideas, modern attitudes and a modern way of speaking Greek. So when I greeted him in the Cypriot dialect and in an uninhibited manner which in fact, was full of warmth and hospitality, his reaction was rather terse.

"Oh" he said, "you speak like a real villager. We don't speak like that in Cyprus anymore. Maybe some old people still do but not the younger generation."

I was a little surprised at his reaction and I felt uncertain about what I should do next. I tried to retain my composure and continued to speak Greek to him because he knew no English. At the same time I was for the first time conscious of how I was speaking Greek. I felt that his comments were an attack on my identity because what is the language that one speaks if it is not what one is? In time it became generally understood by Cypriots that dialect is an enrichment of any language and it should be nurtured and preserved. But this understanding came after some years and particularly after the fall of the Greek Military Junta during the events of 1974. The Junta's ideas were often fascist and incredibly restricted and this included their view that the ancient Greek dialect of Cyprus should be eradicated in preference to the standard Greek that was supposedly spoken in Hellas. I think the experiment failed.

~

Most Cypriot teenagers who had grown up in London joined the teenage revolution. We dressed like our favourite pop singers, we listened to the music of the popular bands of the time and we showed our enthusiasm to succeed socially and educationally. Most of us were becoming very British in language, style, culture and outlook and we were liking it. There may have been some confusing attitudes about how young London Cypriots spoke Greek but there was no confusion about how well we had acquired the English language and how much we were beginning to enjoy living in London.

While young Cypriots were adopting the British popular culture of the time, there was also a feeling of change in Cyprus. Despite the political problems of the island, tourism was beginning to take off. People were beginning to enjoy a higher standard of living and had a lot more money in their pockets. Tourism began to change the narrow village mentality of Cypriots and this was reflected in their life styles and attitude. This happened not suddenly but over a period of years. Change wasn't immediately apparent but it was obvious enough to be noticed by Cypriots from England returning to Cyprus during the late sixties and certainly prior to 1974, to comment how Cyprus had changed and how people were now different - less welcoming, less generous.

Cypriots had also begun to use standard Greek in their every day lives. The influence of television and the wider access to secondary and higher education led to people speaking in what they thought to be a more educated or sophisticated Greek instead of the traditional dialect of Cyprus. London Cypriots, however, continued to speak the Cypriot dialect that they or the their parents had brought with them during the 1950s and 60s before the shift from dialect to standard Greek had begun to take hold amongst the general population of Cyprus. I personally feel that it is rather sad that Cypriots have embraced the evolution from dialect to standard form with such enthusiasm without due regard for a form of Greek that according to legend was brought to Cyprus by Agapenor, an Arcadian, and his followers who on their return voyage from Troy were carried by the winds to Cyprus where they founded the city of Paphos. It must be said that the Cypriot Greek dialect is immensely rich in traditional stories and folk songs and has contributed greatly to the variety and richness of the Greek language. I can only conjuncture that the psychological reason for the willingness of Cypriots to accept such drastic changes in their expression of the Greek language was not only the inevitable influence of the mass media but also because of their age old insecurity of their status as true Hellenes. Perhaps they felt that if you speak like the Athenians you can some how be more Hellenic.

From another point of view, could anyone expect that while the world changed, people in Cyprus should remain static and unchanging? Older Cypriots from England noticed the change more starkly simply because their attitude and cultural outlook remained trapped in the 1950s. Being in England, meant that they could not develop with the host community because of the lack of knowledge of the English language. It also meant that they could not be a part of the cultural changes that were beginning to evolve in Cypriot society. To complicate matters further, young Cypriots in England who had grown up with the strong influence of British culture could not help beginning to forge their identity within the context of their present and immediate environment. There were uncertainties that had to be confronted. If you had been born in England or if you had come to England as a little child and you spoke mainly English, what were you? If you had never been to Cyprus or if most of your experience had been in England, where should you feel that you belonged? Who were your people? What was your identity? These feelings became even more poignant when young Cypriots visited Cyprus and discovered that they spoke in dialect form that was no longer popular with the young people of Cyprus who were now using the standard form of Greek and would sometimes unkindly comment that their Cypriot relatives from England spoke like villagers. Needless to say British Cypriots felt that such comments were unfair and showed a lack of sensitivity.

Nationality

We now have clearer concepts of British nationality and a variety of labels that identify the different ethnic groups that have come to England or have evolved here but this all came later as a response to the new circumstances that emerged with the arrival of millions of new comers to these shores. The people of my generation who came here as children were identified as Cypriot or Greek but the label confused the reality. By the time that I was a teenager I could hardly remember Cyprus and had never been to Greece. The truth is that people like myself were British because we were here and knew no other way of life, had almost no experience other then of England. It was rather uncomfortable to be constantly reminded about being Greek by our parents or by the well intentioned school teachers who wanted to celebrate multiculturalism and who assumed that we were some how experts about the life of people in Cyprus or Greece. There were a few clear thinking people who were able to clarify some of the confusion felt by young Cypriots in search of an identity that they could really accept and say "yes that's us." One such wise individual was Mr Griffin, a teacher at my school. He had been in the RAF during the war and had become an emergency trained teacher after its conclusion. He was a history teacher and had the ability to inspire his students through discussion and the telling of stories about the war based on his real life experiences. On one occasion we got onto the subject of nationality. He asked the group,

"What nationality do you think that you are?"

"I'm British," said my friend Michael."

"I'm Scottish and you'd better not call me British," said another boy.

We all laughed and then Mr Griffin turned to me.

"What nationality are you, Fotis?"

"I'm Greek," I answered instinctively.

Mr. Griffin paused, lowered his tone, spoke kindly, trying not to cause offence.

"No, Fotis. Your nationality is British."

I was surprised by this announcement in front of the class. Mr. Griffin paused and I waited, looking intensely at him. I had always been Greek to everyone around me so what did he mean by this?

"Your nationality, Fotis, is British. You have a Greek ethnicity and you were born in Cyprus but your nationality is British."

I didn't quite understand what the difference was between nationality and ethnicity but Mr Griffin in his calm, cool, and clear manner made me realise that I did not just belong to my Greek past but also to my British present.

Cypriot teenagers who had grown up in London felt the stress of belonging in two camps and when amongst their own families and relatives they expressed their ethnicity through language, music or dance, attending on occasion the Greek Orthodox Church; it was a different matter when they were with friends at school, shopping in Oxford Street or on a night out at a disco. At such times there would occur an ethnic metamorphosis into a Britishness exhibited in fashion, taste in music and amongst other features of the transformation was the fluency in English. These perceptions of identity, these experiments in the presentation of ourselves happened quite naturally and without any preconceived ideas about who we were and what we were trying to become. The process was instinctive and I suppose inevitable and sometimes it was in stark opposition to the aspirations and wishes of our parents who persevered in teaching us our ethnic language when it had become easier and of more benefit to use English both at home and other places.

Arrangement or Romance?

An issue that caused a great deal of tension between young Cypriots who had grown and reached maturity in London and their parents was the choice of marriage partner. The parents almost always wanted their boys to marry Cypriot girls, to speak Greek and to dress smartly but in a conventional manner. Parents and older Cypriots in general mocked what they considered to be the extremes of fashion like long hair or flamboyant clothes for boys or mini skirts and heavy make up for girls. I'm afraid to say that my parents were very disappointed when as a sixth former I grew my hair like many of my school friends and began to dress in flared jeans and floral shirts. My father's teasing had a serious edge to it as he would sometimes comment,

"Fotaki, with your long hair you look like a girl. Go and have a hair cut and dress like a man."

Sometimes we were visited by my sister who was already married and on occasion she was accompanied by her mother and father in-law. Their names were Koumis and Maria. They were both elderly typical Cypriot village people who had very strong Christian values who, in most respects, were full of humour and kindness but they were utterly intolerant of anyone who had a different view of the world from themselves. Hence, when they visited our house and saw me with my long hair and colourful shirt, I immediately become the focus of their attention and the target of their negative remarks.

"You have become like a goat with your hair so long,"

they would say and look away from me and continue to address my mother who often found their company unpleasant.

"You know these long haired people, they are all hashish smokers and you can't trust them."

"My Foti would never do a thing like that, he is far too sensible. He only has long hair because it is the fashion amongst the young people."

My sister's in - laws seemed unconvinced and continued to look at me as if I had just arrived from another planet. My mother always sprung to my defence and after their visit she commented with a smile on her face,

"They really are such thick headed villagers."

After one or two such experiences with my sister's in-laws I quickly vacated the house if I heard that there was an impending visit. Many years after when on holiday in Cyprus, we happened to be in Avgorou from where Koumis and Maria had come from and where they had returned to live. We visited them and they welcomed us with utter warmth. Unexpectedly, just as we were about to get into the car to leave, the now very elderly Maria looked at me and in a very serious manner said,

"I am so glad, Foti, that you have cut that horrible long hair. Now you smell like a real man."

I thanked her for her hospitality, a little surprised that the issue of boys growing their hair long in keeping with the fashion of the time had been so significant for her.

.

The Cypriot parents who made the journey to England as adults and whose children were either born or were raised in England did not think that their children would be different from them. They imagined that the new generation would be as Cypriot as they were but alas, how could this be? The parents were to be disappointed in their expectations and one of the issues that clearly pointed to the difference between the older generation and their anglicised children was the arranged marriage. For the parents it was unthinkable that their children should not go through the process of the traditional arranged marriage. There was certainly much friction in families regarding this matter but eventually it was the parents who lost the battle and surrendered to the inevitable. Their children eventually broke this particular tradition and claimed their right to have choice about who they married. Cypriots adopted the "romantic" relationship as a means to choosing their marriage partner and, of course, we all know that romance does not recognize differences in race or creed. Cypriots of both sexes began to marry outside of the community and though at first this seemed rather uncomfortable, over a span of a few years it had become acceptable and quite normal. The success in breaking out of the ethnic cocoon and recognizing that you cannot live in a narrow existence imported from elsewhere is an important step in the development of ethnic communities, living either here or elsewhere in the world.

For the Cypriot community it has not meant that it is less Cypriot; it merely showed that we were also more British and beginning to feel more comfortable with our new environment and the new way of life.

Enoch

In the late 1960s the notion of multiculturalism gathered pace. Its intention was to celebrate diversity in British society and to teach particularly children to respect each others language, culture, religion and way of life. It was felt by liberal minded people that there was a need for British society to change and to educate itself in response to the new social conditions of a population that almost over night had changed in composition and would continue to do so in the years ahead. This was an appropriate response to right wing populist politicians who gambled on furthering their careers by playing the race card.

One such political figure was Enoch Powel who said that the British were " mad" to accept so many alien people into these islands and prophesised that there would be "rivers of blood" implying that there would be some kind of apocalyptic conflict between the British people and the new arrivals. 'The Rivers of Blood' speech was Enoch Powell's response to increasing immigration to this country and to the anti-discrimination laws that had been introduced. Interestingly, it is likely that this speech by Powell who was an MP for the Conservative Party in opposition is thought to have contributed to the surprise Conservative Party general election victory of 1970 which brought Edward Heath to power. From this result we can see many British people may, indeed, have been sympathetic to Enoch Powell's view on immigration.

The speech itself was directed at "the ordinary Englishman". Its purpose was to warn him or her of the consequences of large scale immigration to this country. It presented the immigrants as people who would take over the land, pushing the English population to one side. The speech had the obvious intention of instilling fear and panic in ordinary citizens. It was also intended to provoke action in order to prevent the supposed takeover of the land by alien people. Here is an example from the speech:

"We must be mad as a nation to be permitting the annual inflow of some 50,000 dependents who for the most part are material for the future growth of the immigrant descendent population. It is like watching a nation busily engaged in heaping up its own funeral pyre. So insane are we that we actually permit unmarried persons to immigrate for the purpose of founding a family with spouses and fiancées who they have never seen." [1]

In an opinion poll taken by the Gallop Poll Organisation it was found that 74% of people questioned agreed with the views expressed in Enoch Powell's speech. [2]

Father couldn't help picking up bits of information about what was going on. He detested Edward Heath because he was the Conservative Prime Minister and in my father's eyes the leader of the wealthy classes. But father also understood that politicians like Edward Heath and Harold Wilson whom my father greatly admired were very different from this Enoch Powell who was hardly known before his racist and inflammatory speech. His "Rivers of blood" speech was shown on the television news with what appeared to be large scale support from the public. When my father saw this he became rather worried and anxiously questioned me about it.

"What is he saying about us?" asked my father.

I didn't quite understand Enoch Powell's use of imagery but my father comprehended the meaning very clearly.

"What else is he saying?" father persisted.

"I think he is saying that there are too many immigrants here in England and soon there will not be any place for English people to live. I think he is saying that we should all get out of England."

My father then exploded.

"Who does he think, this terrible man? He is like another Hitler! The Labour Party will never allow this to happen!"

Father had faith that good would triumph over evil and in this case good was represented by the Labour Party who would deal with the incredibly evil Enoch Powell. Mother, however, was not as confident that this problem would be dealt with by what my father called people of good will.

"Loizo, these people do not want us here in their country."

She spoke quietly and with a perplexed expression on her face.

"Can't you see," she continued, "that many of them look at us with contempt, make comments at us in the streets. Now they are marching with flags and banners. They have a leader and they are following him. Are you sure that we and our children are safe here?"

After mother had spoken for a few minutes there was a silence in the room as if we were all taking in the significance of the moment.

"We will be alright," my father broke in reassuringly but mother was unconvinced. For her this really was a time of uncertainty and she often talked about returning to Cyprus despite the problems that she would find there.

~

The British liberal establishment kicked back by launching multiculturalism to run as a major theme in education and in the defining policies of all public British institutions. This was the powerful response of the liberal establishment to the evil of racism and for the most immediate needs it certainly worked. The school curriculum was revised to reflect Britain as a multicultural society. Black culture and black history was introduced as was the study of world religions. Black and Asian people became a common phenomenon on television and in areas of responsibility. I am not saying that all problems based on race disappeared over night or that as a result of multiculturalism we had succeeded in transforming Britain into some kind of utopia that was devoid of racism and prejudice. But without a doubt multiculturalism improved the understanding that people of different races living in this country had of each other. But all this had yet to be achieved. Meanwhile Enoch Powell's speech had created immediate tension on the streets. There were almost instant demonstrations by the dock workers who on the 23rd of April 1970 went on strike, marching to the Palace of Westminster to protest against the sacking of Powell from the cabinet by Edward Heath. They carried placards that declared "Back Britain, not Black Britain". Leading political figures on the whole condemned the speech as inflammatory and damaging to race relations. But Enoch Powell was not without support amongst the political elite. Margaret Thatcher, an important member of the government and future prime minister, called his speech "strong meat",[3] expressing reluctance to support actions against him.

~

As a result of the Powell's speech, there was an increase in racist abuse in the streets. Some times my parents came home from work and exclaimed their outrage at having been called "bloody foreigners" or when they were rudely told to "go back to where you come from" .The xenophobia that had been deliberately unleashed by this opportunist demagogue also extended into the school where English school children adopting and learning the attitudes of their parents and elders began a bullying campaign against immigrant children. Cypriot children were victimised and called names: "Greek bubbles" or "Greek bastards". Some English students formed into gangs and attacked us or other ethnic minority children for no other reason then for being of a different colour or race. We often moved around the school in real fear of attack from these young racist. Some immigrant children were so fearful that they refused to go to school. They would set off for school in the morning but never arrived. Instead they walked around the streets, rode on the tube or went to the cinema.

In huge contrast to the conditions of today in which it is common to find an anti racist policy in the prospectus and mission statement of any school in the United Kingdom, the teachers at that time just did not know what to do or how to react in response to the monster of racism that had reared its head in their midst. It was to be sometime before educators and teachers would themselves fully understand the problem of racism and introduce effective programmes in the education curriculum to fight ingrained racist attitudes.

Luckily, the direct hostility engendered by Powell's speech did not overtly endure and people, with the passing of time, were able to address the problems presented by a society in a state of flux. My father, after all, was right. People of goodwill did not allow Enoch Powell and his racist followers to succeed. In time, though even now it has not entirely disappeared, most of the racist verbal abuse on the streets faded away. The teddy boy and later the skin head hostility and violence towards ethnic minorities was never very wide spread and it also came to an end. Without a doubt education had a great deal to do with combating racism in the United Kingdom but more then this, it was the common sense, the moderate attitude and the sense of fair play of the majority of people in the United Kingdom that enabled a multicultural society to evolve.

Waiting for the Bus

Not long after the "rivers of blood" speech I experienced a disturbing incident on the streets of London. I had not long completed my "A" level GCE examinations and having gone through the rigours of three months of intensive revision followed by some very tough examinations, my fellow students and I were all very keen to put this trying experience behind us and have a good time. It happened that on one particular Saturday night I had been invited to a party by one of my friends from school whose parents were away for the weekend. He lived in a large Victorian house in Camden Mews, just off Camden Road. I had arrived at about 9pm and the party was already in full swing. Most of the people present were from the sixth form of Highbury School. Every one was looking trendy. The girls were in mini skirts and the boys all had long hair with patterned shirts that had unusually big collars. The music was loud and rhythmic. There was a tasty choice: The Rolling Stones sang their greatest hit "Here comes my 19th nervous break down," and The Kinks oozed with London sophistication with "Dedicated follower of fashion." There were hits by The Animals and lots of music by my favourite, Cat Stevens.

There was a lot of drink and some of the guests were already rather merry and dancing in the middle of the living room. Our host, whose name was Andreas, a fellow Greek Cypriot had gone to the trouble of creating a real party atmosphere by setting up multicoloured lights that flashed while the music blared loudly from the latest stereophonic music centre. The doorbell rang every five minutes. Some people were leaving early while others had only just arrived. There were people everywhere: some were sitting on the staircase, others occupied the corridor. Inside the living room the lights had been dimmed and couples were dancing with their arms tightly wound around each other. There was laughter and loud talking. The house was full of cigarette smoke but in those days nobody seemed to care.

I felt relaxed and good about myself because I had completed my "A" levels and now was the time to celebrate. After a couple of beers I lit up a cigarette just to look cool in front of some of the girls. When I inhaled I thought of how angry mother would be with me if she saw me with a cigarette in my mouth. I tried to push the thought out of my mind. Eventually, I danced around with some of friends for a while and then I had some more beer and was really enjoying myself. It was then that quite by chance I happened to look at the little carriage clock on the mantle shelf. When I looked carefully at it, I realised that it was time for me to leave. The time was 12.45 and the last bus along Camden Road would be going by at approximately 1 a.m.

"Andreas, I've gotta go now, gotta catch the last bus. Great party, see ya later, mate!"

Andreas looked up from the pretty girl he was embracing.

"Hey, Foti, why ya going so early for? The party's only just starting."

A friend called out teasingly,

"Mummy will be angry, Foti, if you're not home by the deadline," then they all broke out in loud laughter.

I had already opened the front door to exit before they could continue with their silly jokes. They liked to tease and I didn't mind because they were my friends. I closed the door behind me and walked down the quiet mews towards the main road.

I felt the cool air drying the perspiration on my forehead. I had had a very good time and it had been a real pleasure to see my friends from school. Walking at a brisk pace while humming to myself the Cat Stevens hit "I love my dog as much as I love you," I soon reached the bus stop that was situated outside the gates of the Jewish Free School along Camden Road.

There was another person at the bus stop waiting for the last bus. It was a pretty young woman, probably the same age as me or even a little younger. She was standing very still and had quite a serious expression on her face. She made no attempt to speak or look in my direction so we both waited quietly, looking in the direction from where we expected the night bus to appear. There was a gentle, warm breeze that made the night feel cool and refreshing. An occasional motor car would go by from time to time. A dog could be heard barking some where in the distance. Everything seemed full of peace and tranquillity. The girl and I, now hardly aware of each other, stood at the bus stop, breathing in the cool night air, waiting for the bus.

We had not been long at the bus stop when suddenly there was a loud commotion to be heard coming in our direction. The peace and quiet had suddenly been disturbed. Having turned off from one of the side roads we could see four young men heading in our direction. They were kicking an empty beer can around and shouted obscene remarks at passing motorists. They laughed in an exaggerated manner and screamed at the top of their voices. The girl and I looked in their direction and then for a moment, feeling alarmed, at each other. There was no one else around except for the four rowdy individuals who were drawing closer and closer to us with every passing second.

When the rowdy gang of four noticed the young woman and me at the bus stop they become suddenly very quiet. They briefly stopped, looked, said something to each other and then proceeded towards us. I couldn't help feeling that there was going to be a problem. I looked again down the road for any sign of the bus but unfortunately there was no sign of any.

Before long, the gang had reached the bus stop and had strategically placed themselves between me and the girl.

I couldn't help noticing that the members of the gang were dressed in smart jeans and shirts. They didn't look thuggish but it was obvious that they had been drinking. I was hopeful that nothing unpleasant was going to happen. The young woman looked composed and hadn't been panicked by their stares. They remained silent for a couple of minutes while they stared at the girl in a cold manner that must have made her feel very uncomfortable while they showed no interest towards me. I stood still and silent, trying to look indifferent and as if nothing was amiss. Then they started.

One of them approached the girl and stood very close to her. He breathed right into her face and looking at her directly in the eyes with a silly smirk, said,

"Well, I've seen lots of girls tonight but you must be the sexiest."

He turned and grinned at his on lookers while they grinned back and egged him on. In his stupidity he probably felt that the girl found him and his approach irresistible. The girl retained her composure and calmly ignoring him turned to one side looking out towards the road. Her message was clear that she didn't want to be bothered. His friends and audience burst out laughing at him.

"She ain't interested in you," said one while the other joined in,

"Better luck next time!"

They jeered and laughed at him. The jilted suitor stood there not knowing how to respond then one of his friends stepped forward and said,

"Step aside and look at how it's done by a master."

"Go on John, whooooah!"

Two of them called out while the failed suitor looked on to see if his friend could do better then him.

His friends continued to snigger at him because what he had said must have highlighted even to them how foolish he actually sounded. He then approached the girl from behind while she was looking blankly across the road and grabbed her arm, violently swung her round to face him. He tried to grab her by the waist and to kiss her on the lips. In her panic the girl screamed and struggled against her assailant.

"What ya doin! Are ya crazy! Leave me alone, will ya! I'll call a cop if ya don't watch out," she threatened hopelessly but at that moment in time it seemed that all the night buses and all the policemen in the world had suddenly disappeared.

I wasn't surprised by the verbal abuse of these individuals but at that moment I was shocked by the physical attack on the girl. It was time to do something. I knew that I would end up getting a beating because all four of them were big guys but I Just could not help myself.

"Please! Leave her alone! She's frightened!"

My intervention seemed feeble even to me and I was fully aware of the possible consequences. All at once, as if I had rudely reminded them of my existence, they turned and faced me. The girl realising that I was her only protection on the deserted scene ran and stood behind me. She was shocked and frightened. All her detached composure had evaporated as she clutched to the back of my jacket. I could also see that the gang of four were very intoxicated. Their eyes were blood shot and their faces full of hostility because I had dared to intervene in their proceedings. The self assured one who had been embarrassed by the girl came towards me with glaring, red eyes and growled at me through clenched teeth as if his jaw had been stapled together.

"Are ya talking to me, ya little Greek bastard! Are ya talking to me!" he repeated as if in outraged disbelief. Meanwhile, the other members of the gang like a hunting pack began to encircle. Their fists were clenched and they were ready to pounce.

"I was just saying that you're frightening her.....there's no need," but I was the one who was now really frightened.

With this they became even more infuriated and seemed to be on the verge of a mad assault.

"Who ya tellin what to do, ya Greek bastard...I'm gonna break your legs before Enoch sends ya home! I'm gonna cripple ya!" They were building their anger into a frenzy.

The girl and I stood there frightened. We didn't know what to do. We expected the worst. They roared and screamed abuse but there was no attack. Perhaps, they had not as yet developed their true violent potential which is often typical of racist thugs and despite my sense of panic and fear at that moment, something that my would be assailant said echoed in my mind.

"...before Enoch sends ya home...before Enoch sends ya home."

"Ya Greek bastard!" another one yelled and pushed me so that I staggered backwards, crashing into the girl who was standing behind me. The image of the teacher with the thin red lips suddenly and unexpectedly flashed across my mind.

"That will teach you a lesson!" she sneered with her red rouged lips. Then the old man with the bowler hat in an instant flashed across my mind.

"Enoch's gonna break your legs, ya Greek bastard!" growled the nasty old man. The girl's voice suddenly brought me back to my senses.

"Look, the bus is coming!" She shouted into my ear while helping me back on to my feet.

Unexpectedly, the late night bus appeared as if out of thin air. In the confusion of what was happening, the bus had approached the stop. The driver must have sensed what was going on. It was our chance to make an escape. Instinctively, I grabbed the girl's hand and we both jumped onto the platform of the route master. Before the gang of four, in their drunken stupor could respond, the West Indian bus conductor had rung the bell and the bus drove off, leaving the four thugs stranded on the Camden Road.

"It look like ya having some problem with those guys," said the bus conductor with a Caribbean accent and a friendly smile on his face.

"Na," I said, "they were just a bit drunk. Nothing we couldn't handle," I said with a laugh, trying to look cool about the whole matter. But the girl and I both knew that it could have ended very badly for us, we'd had a lucky escape.

In the safety and warmth of the bus we sat together, talking and feeling relieved that we had escaped from those thugs. Just before she got off at Holloway Road, she embraced and kissed me on the cheek.

"Thanks, I was really scared and you were very brave. See ya around."

She was really stunningly beautiful and I always hoped that I would run into her somewhere or other but unfortunately it did not happen. I never saw her again. But one thing is for certain, I think that like myself, she will always remember the night when we waited together for the late night bus.

A happy ending you might think that remained a fond memory but also because eventually the racist demagogy of Enoch Powel was not bought by the vast majority of the British people and Enoch as a politician very soon sank into oblivion and was only revered by a small number of fanatics who maintained that he had the gift of prophecy.

~

It may have surprised Enoch and his followers but most people were willing to learn about each different cultures and traditions and to be enriched by this experience. It was a slow process, an evolvement in the understanding of new circumstances in society. The media was another powerful tool through which white, Anglo-Saxon society was influenced into a more positive way of thinking about people of a different race or/and colour. There were films like "To Sir with Love" starring Sidney Poitier as a new black teacher in, who arrives at a London secondary school and is faced by white students, who are very hostile to him because of his colour. The film is about how the hostile, white racist students learn that black is beautiful and that their black teacher is a caring individual who has the talent to help them develop as human beings. Alongside Sidney Poitier was the very young Lulu who played in the role of one of the young, unruly and prejudiced teenagers that created a headache for their new black teacher. As the plot of the film unfolds she and her friends learn that people should be judged for their values and not by the colour of their skin. The theme song to the film was also performed by Lulu. It was one of her best songs and remains a haunting reminder of our early attempts to tackle the ugliness of racism. I remember going to the cinema with my friends to see this film. At the end of the film we emerged from the cinema smiling because of the happy ending but also aware and influenced by the film's message of love and respect for each other. There were other films with similar content and message. Also at this time black and brown faces were becoming more common on television.

Today, we know that in certain respects this feature of multiculturalism has worked quite well because, on the whole, people stopped noticing that a news presenter like Trevor McDonald is black but rather appreciated his professional delivery of the news to a nationwide audience. This was possible due to the ability of the majority of the people to take on the changes in society and to respond in a fair and balanced manner. This has enabled ethnic minority people to express their talents in a very broad area of national life including business, industry, medicine, the arts, sport, the armed forces and so on. Has British society and culture not benefitted by the influx of people from the Commonwealth and from other parts of the world? People like the late Enoch Powell with his apocalyptic visions of "rivers of blood" and others of his ilk have been proved quite mistaken in their projections because the voice of justice, fairness and moderation, have prevailed.

The arranged marriage

My sister Kika did not achieve her academic potential. Instead, like most young women of her background, while still in her teens was faced with the arranged marriage.

The weddings were an outward symbol, they showed a community that was well ordered, prosperous and while settling into its new country of abode it continued to emphasize the importance of its ancient customs and traditions. It seems that life was more straightforward for the young women who had arrived in England in their late teens and who therefore identified more strongly with the way of life of the older generation of Cypriots.

It was not so simple for the girls who had arrived as young children or who were born here in the United Kingdom and attended schools in London or some other British city. These "British Cypriots" faced the impact of the fashions, styles, the ideas and attitudes of British teenagers who were involved in their own teenage revolution facilitated by increasing wealth and influenced by new ideas and developments in society. The birth control pill had been introduced and would be a catalyst for change. It was a sexual revolution that ended the notion of the subservient woman who would go from being a daughter to being a wife. Feminism had re- emerged from its slumber and with a more powerful voice. Perhaps the politician who reflected the spirit of the time was Roy Jenkins in his speech in which he referred to "the permissive society". This memorable phrase implied many thing s including the right of women to belong to themselves and not to any other master as dictated by custom or religion.

These ideas entered the consciousness of young ethnic minority women who had grown up in the United Kingdom, had attended school with British teenagers and had observed them enjoying a life style and freedom that was denied to them. My sister Kika was one such a teenager who had the possibility of living a very different life from that which was planned by our parents. She was, I know uncomfortable with the idea of an arranged marriage but at the age of seventeen she did not have the voice to resist parents and the powerful force of tradition. When my sister had hardly turned sixteen, our parents began to introduce the subject of getting engaged.

Sometimes mother would utter very softly,

"You are sixteen years old already, Kika. Soon a handsome young man from a good family will see you at a wedding party or at the church and then it will be your turn to marry."

Our parents spoke kindly to her about this matter as if they were trying to persuade a child to do something that the child could not really understand. Then mother who was more practical then father would add,

"Not just someone in tight trousers who will gamble and drink. Such men are a waste of time. Your future husband should have a trade and be a good worker."

As mother spoke these words to my sister, she looked at her with immense love and pride but there was also a hint of worry in her look and uncertainty in her voice.

Kika wouldn't argue with our parents even if she didn't like what they were saying; then she would become very quiet and sullen. I understood that she was unhappy about marrying so young but she had been brought up to be an obedient girl. In Cypriot tradition it was demanded that girls should be obedient daughters and then obedient wives. She had never been encouraged to ask questions, to disagree or to express an opinion that was contrary to tradition. Even though the obedient attitude was encouraged from childhood and became a part of the fibre of the personality, on one occasion Kika found the courage to speak her thoughts.

"I don't want to get married so young," she protested. I want to go to a school where I can learn hairdressing and then I want to work for a while. It's too early for me to marry."

Our parents were amused by Kika's outburst which was perhaps worse then if they had become angry. It just meant that they were not taking Kika's feelings into any consideration. Mother tried to reason with Kika by explaining what had been explained to herself when she was no more than a child by her own mother.

"It is right for a woman to marry early," she spoke persuasively.

"You will have a husband , your own home , children, nothing is more important. What good is school? You can be lead astray in such places. A woman can acquire a bad reputation if she is unmarried for too long."

While mother was speaking these words she appeared uncomfortable and even unconvinced by her own argument. Father then put an end to the discussion.

"Kika , we deeply love and care for you. You are very precious to us. No one has a better daughter and we are proud of you but on this issue your mother is right. This is how your grandmothers married.

This is how your mother and I married and this is how you will marry. This is how the world is."

Kika listened to father's words and then looked down at the floor without answering. I knew that she disagreed with father but she would not argue with him. In later life she spoke about how unfair it was that she should have married so young and against her true feelings but she also expressed the understanding that mother and father did what they thought was best for her.

There was a formal process for the arranged marriage: the 'proxenetis' or the proposer acted on behalf of the young man and his family. He consulted with the family of the young woman regarding the possibility of introducing the young people for the purpose of marriage. This was followed by an initial meeting in which the parents of the couple discussed the matter. It was important at this meeting to go through, as sincerely as possible, everything that needed to be spoken about. It was a bad idea to try to withhold information that if it came to light could have an adverse effect on the future marriage. If all went well, the young man and woman had a first meeting accompanied by their families and they had a chance to see each other.

This is how events occurred in my sister's road to marriage. We were first visited by the Proxenetis with the father of the young man. They were welcomed to our home and they sat with my father in the living room where they talked. My mother made coffee and served it to the men then sat quietly and listened to the men discussing the matter. At the beginning, the conversation was informal but then the important questions were asked. These related to the age of the couple, their jobs, their characters and what help each would receive from their family.

"My son is a strong young man who does not shy away from work. He will work hard to support a wife and children."

By this he meant that his son would have to stand on his own feet and not expect financial help from him. Then it was my father's turn to speak about what he was able to offer.

"My daughter," he began, "is an able and hard working girl who can earn good wages working as a seamstress. I can also help by allowing them to have a room in our flat and live here without contributing money so that they can save for the future."

This was my father's way of saying that my sister had no dowry. Eventually the person, who all this discussion was about, was called to the room with the pretext of asking her to make some more coffee. My sister entered looking shy and embarrassed. She was seventeen years old and in many respects no more then a child.

"This is our daughter Kika." My father introduced her with pride and one could see a father's love in the expression on his face.

"Would you make us some more coffee, Kika," my father added.

"Yes father," she answered obediently while all the time looking down and feeling too shy to meet anyone's eyes.

All went well at this first meeting. My father and our guest agreed that the two families should meet together so that the two young people should have a chance to see each other.

When the time came, the two families gathered together, the men were talking in one group while the women were conversing in another. Nobody spoke about the reason for the gathering, everyone acted as if they were devoid of such knowledge but every one knew the real reason and so the members of the young man's family were unobtrusively and kindly observing my sister. On the other hand, mother was watching the young man like a hawk, trying to discover signs of any habits that might indicate that he would not be a suitable husband for my sister.

The custom was that after a day or so, the young people involved, were asked if they really liked each other and if they were willing to marry. If both agreed then matters went to the next stage. This was the formal 'logiasma' or the giving of the word of promise. Though it appeared to be fair that both young people were consulted if they wanted to proceed in the matter, the nature of this arrangement coupled with the traditional village values of the parents must have meant that girls were exposed to coercion. I know that though my sister had already said that she didn't want to go through with it, matters were presented to her in such a manner, particularly by father, that when it came to giving her answer, she was unable to refuse.

A short while after the "logisma" or the giving of the promise, the engagement was arranged. At this ceremony a priest was invited to bless the engaged couple and to bless their engagement rings. The celebration was usually quite a big event to which friends and relatives were invited but it was the wedding, of course, that was the culmination of the events which were set in motion by the proxenetis enquiry.

The planning for the wedding took place almost immediately after the engagement. Dates were arranged, the church and reception hall would be booked. Invitations were printed out on very ornate cards and usually in gold print. For my sister's wedding the invitation read:

'Mr. and Mrs. Loizou from Sotira, Famagusta, Cyprus and Mr. and Mrs. Ataou from Avgorou, Famagusta, Cyprus request the pleasure of your company at the wedding of their children Kika and George at All Saints Greek Orthodox Church.'

The number of guests was in the hundreds and each family was visited personally to be presented with the invitation from the couple or their parents. Such a custom wasn't a problem in a small village in Cyprus but it was quite an undertaking if you lived in London. Yet, most families who planned the weddings of their children went through this laborious process of zigzagging across London to deliver the invitations.

My sister's wedding was typical of many. The couple went through the ancient ceremony standing before the altar. The church of All Saints in Pratt Street, Camden Town was crowded with men, women and children. Everyone was dressed in their best clothes. The men wore dark suits with stiffly starched white shirts with colourful ties. The women wore eye catching dresses, high heeled shoes with pointed toes. The witnesses, the koumpari and the koumeres stood in a circle around the alter with the bride and groom at the apex. The Orthodox Priests in their richly embroidered Byzantine cassocks busied themselves singing the marriage liturgy that seemed to go on forever. The icons of the Twelve Apostles, forever frozen in their silent postures, looked down from the iconostasis as the couple were joined together in matrimony.

Following the religious ceremony, all travelled by car or coach to the reception hall which was the local town hall. The catering was prepared at home. Both families worked through the previous night at home to cook and then to deliver great quantities of meat balls, roasted chicken, salads and such usual dips as tahini, houmous and taramosalata. The tables were set with bottles of wine and whiskey and with an abundance of food. A live band with violin, bouzuki and drums entertained and went through a list of songs and dances which like every Cypriot wedding culminated in the dance of the bride and bridegroom when the guests pinned money on them.

While the bride and bride groom celebrated their nuptial their guests saw it as an opportunity to seek out friends and relatives at the party. It was a great get together where people ate, drank, danced but most of all they talked and talked about their families and work, life in England or the Cyprus problem. Often it was a chance to catch up on the latest gossip. This is how so many Greek Cypriot men and women were married in London during the late 50s and 60s. With the increasing sophistication and the growing wealth of the community, this traditional village type wedding went through quite a change.

The young women who went through this process are now the mothers of grown up children who are themselves parents. Most of these grandmothers share the common experience of the arranged marriage, and will also, probably, if they are not too embarrassed, confirm that on the morning after their wedding, the elders of the two families would inspect the bridal bed sheets to examine the proof that the bride had indeed been pure and a virgin on her wedding night. I remember very clearly on that morning how my sister's in-laws had arrived at our house very early.

Together with my parents, they entered the bedroom of the newly married couple .They were very composed because this was for them a very serious matter. When they remerged they were full of smiles and happy tears. They hugged and kissed my sister who smiled back at them but seemed very uncomfortable and embarrassed by the whole process. From the point of view of these village people, family honour had been maintained and enhanced because the daughter had been given in marriage as a pure virgin and they had the evidence to prove it.

Thankfully for most of us, life has changed for the better and certainly the young women from our community now marry when they like and whom they like. I am happy that the Cypriots have learnt that there should be limits to certain traditions but sadly there are other communities in the United Kingdom who have not yet understood that their young people who have been born or have been raised here question and often are against the idea of the arranged marriage .

Tulay

How strange it must have seemed to the girls who had grown up in the United Kingdom and who had tasted the new permissive British culture to be expected to go through an arranged village marriage and worse still to be subjected to the post wedding night examination! Further, this is not yesterday's injustice inflicted on the young women of ethnic minority groups of long ago. We are not only speaking of young women who have recently arrived to the United Kingdom from far away villages in Pakistan or India. British teenagers often from Islamic backgrounds are taken for "holidays" to India or Pakistan and when they arrive there they are faced with an arranged marriage often to a complete stranger. Some teenagers feel that they have to choose between the traditions of their families and their own new values that belong to the culture of the country that they now live in and think of as their own. It is a difficult choice but some ethnic minority young women find the courage to make it. In some horrific cases the families concerned will take matters to the extreme and inflict upon the rebellious young woman, as they see it, the ultimate punishment of death, justifying their obscene actions by claiming that the behaviour of their victim had brought dishonour upon the family.

One such tragic case related to Tulay Goren who had belonged to the Kurdish community from Turkey. In 1999 when she was only fifteen years old she went missing. Her father was eventually arrested and tried for her murder. During the trial it was revealed that Tulay had fallen in love with a man that the family did not approve of and when she failed not only to terminate the relationship but also ran away to live with her lover, the family decided to take action.

She was enticed back to the family home where she was immediately made a prisoner. Her father Mehmet Goren bound her with a washing line rope and she was badly beaten. The father then ordered his wife and children to go to relatives. When they returned Tulay was no longer there and she has not been seen since. In a dramatic and sensational trial in which Hanim Goren testified against her husband, Mehmet Goren, the father of the victim was found guilty of Tulay's murder.

Trying to apply traditional village "honour" customs from far away cultures to the complex circumstances of ethnic minority British teenagers growing and developing in London has proved to be in some cases explosive and disastrous, particularly for the young people concerned. In the United Kingdom today there are hundreds of cases of women mainly from Asian background who have disappeared and are thought to be, like Tulay Goren, victims of honour killings.

These events illustrate the inability of some members of a community or family to change and to live in accordance to the laws of the society in which they have chosen to live in. Given the chance, Mehmet Goran would argue that his daughter had broken the unwritten laws of tradition and that she had to be punished. This is what he might say:

"We are Kurds from eastern Turkey. We had to leave our village and our homes because there were so many problems there. When we came here we brought our way of life with us. Even though we are here, we didn't suddenly stop being Kurds. We will never do that. We are different from western people and our values are different. Here in London we can see how terrible the women behave. They do not have honour. They dress without modesty and they go with different men all the time. To me, they are like prostitutes with no one to control them. But I did not care about them. My concern was for my family. I was determined that my wife and daughters would behave with honour. I didn't want to be disgraced by them. My wife is mine and so are my daughters until they marry; they have to obey me and not allow themselves to be corrupted by any man. I didn't make these rules. This is how we are taught by our fathers, this is our tradition, this is our way of life and it can't be questioned. Then Tulay decided to turn our world up side down. She had been badly influenced at school and what she saw in the streets. She did not have the common sense to maintain her dignity and honour. She disobeyed and shamed us by going with a man that we did not approve of. My family honour was damaged. I was left with no alternative. Our tradition tells us that a disobedient woman who compromises her honour must be punished. There was nothing else I could do. She had to pay for what she had done."

I can imagine how Tulay would shake her head in disagreement at her father's words. If she could she would explain her point of view about what she had done. This is perhaps what she might say:

"As a child I always listened to my mother and father. We are Kurds and Kurdish girls are taught from infancy to first obey their parents and then when they marry to obey their husbands. For the women in the villages of Kurdistan there is no other life. They go from their father's house to their husband's house without knowing anything else except obedience to father or to husband. I am not saying that this is alright, that it is acceptable for women to live in such bondage but it is easier to live in such conditions if you don't know any better, if you have never experienced any other way of life. But it was very different for me. I came to England as a child. I grew up here and I went to an English school. I had friends who were allowed to dress how they pleased, to wear make up and to have friends who were boys. It seemed natural and a part of growing up in a normal way. Why should I have been denied these rights that my friends enjoyed? My father once explained that we are Kurdish Moslems and it is our custom for the women to stay at home and to be obedient to their husbands and fathers. At school we were taught something different, that women have equal rights with men and that they should work hard to reach their full potential. One of my teachers once said to me that women can do much more then just marry and have children. She said that women should try to gain a good education, travel , have a profession and by doing some of these things they can become not only better wives and mothers but also stronger human beings. I listened carefully to my teacher's words. My teachers presented me with a different view of how my life could be lived. I also listened to my friends who were planning their future. Some said that they would go to university or that they would travel. Others explained how they wanted to meet a man that they could really love, a man of their own choice to make their lives together. When my friends at school spoke about these things I kept very quiet because I felt that I could not be a part of such hopes. It is then that I began to feel that it was unfair for me to stay at home all the time or that I would not have the chance to marry who I wanted. My father talked to me as if we had never left our village in the mountains. In the end I realised that I would have to challenge the traditional views of my father. I feared my father's wrath but it was something I was prepared to face. The threat of beatings could no longer deter me from the deep longing to become a free person."

The story of Tulay's tragic fate may remind us that tradition isn't written in stone. It is in the nature of people to challenge that which is no longer relevant to them and to reach out for new meanings in their lives. No amount of threat, bullying, coercion or violence will succeed in halting the natural desire of the young to be a part of the society in which they live. It is an inevitable and unstoppable process. The women and the girls who are kept under the thumb of male authoritarian circumstances eventually find their voice. The Cypriots like the Kurds also felt that a woman belonged to a father or a husband, that they should be modest, quiet and responsible for the children and the home. My mother could not challenge these assumptions nor could my sister find the voice of protest against the injustice that men inflicted upon women. But the new generation of women in the Cypriot community have been making up for lost ground. Many of them have chosen their own husbands. They are now not only wives and mothers but also university graduates, entrepreneurs, successful in every walk of life and often the pride of their families.

The Mother Tongue

Boys from the Greek Cypriot community did not face the same problems as their sisters. Boys like me, who had come to England as young children were after a few years well on the way to becoming anglicized. The most apparent sign of this in relation to myself was that my use of English after the age of about twelve or thirteen had already become fluent, rich and expressive while my use of the Greek Language had remained static and clumsy. For me and my Greek friends who had arrived together as very young children, English had now become our every day language and we spoke it in school, on the streets and where ever we gathered together to play. Our parents were uncertain how they should face this sudden new phenomenon. For some strange reason they had not bargained that their young children would be fluent speakers of English and at best only second rate speakers of Greek. They had probably naively thought that we would grow up as typical Cypriots right in the middle of London, oblivious to the life around us. Well, they were soon to be disappointed and it is a lesson that still needs to be learnt by those who have only recently arrived and who fanatically wish to enforce the customs and rules of far away places on the children who are being raised in England. So when our parents would look upon us at social gatherings, speaking English in a strong and confident manner while at the same time responding to them in the type of Greek that only a foreign person would utter, they often exclaimed,

"Speak in your own language as well, otherwise you will forget it."

They said this in a semi worried, semi amused tone and of course they already understood that the first serious loss of identity when you live as an ethnic minority far from your own shores is your language. This may happen in stages and it may take a generation or two but as surely as night follows day, it is one of the conclusions of moving from one country to another. There are a thousand and one reasons why we, the Cypriots, who came here as children or who were born here do not retain the old mother language. It might be worth mentioning some of those reasons.

The English language is phenomenally powerful and at the same time easy to acquire. What made it very attractive for youngsters coming to live in England and of course to other people in general is the fact that it is the language of the powerful American film industry. All the world famous film stars from the beginning of film making have been English speaking. In films cowboys and Red Indians spoke in English, Roman emperors and pharaohs, gladiators and slave girls, detectives and hoods, ladies, heroes of romance, comedians and dancers alike all spoke in English. To understand the films you have to understand the language. There were other incentives: the songs of popular music were sang mainly in English and of course our instincts motivated us to learn the language of the place for ordinary, every day reasons like going to school, making friends and having a social life. It wasn't long before we were even thinking in English. What other outcome could there possibly be?

The Change

It was more then fifty years ago that we embarked on a ship from a small picturesque port in Cyprus. We were a simple group of people, a family beginning a journey to England like many other families before us and as many others would do so after us. We were like a small wave, a part of a more general movement of people not only from Cyprus but from other parts of the world in search of a better future, in search of a destiny that might provide hope and fulfilment of dreams. It is quite wonderful and restores some of our lost faith in the face of what is often a cruel world that some rich and powerful countries recognized the need to embrace the poor and the oppressed from troubled or devastated areas of the world. I know that some will say that it was not out of kindness and that these countries wanted cheap labour to feed their economies. That is true but it must also be said that the immigrants were granted democratic rights. We became citizens, we had the right to vote, we could participate in education, in business, in the professions. We were offered hope when often in our own war torn lands we had none. In the sonnet composed by Emma Lazarus and which inscribes the Statue of Liberty, we read the following:

> Give me your tired, your poor,
> Your huddled masses yearning to be free,
> the wretched refuse of your teeming shores.
> Send these, the homeless, tempest-tossed to me,

I lift my lamp beside the golden door.

Were we not the tired and the poor? Were we not homeless and tempest tossed? Yes, we were, but typical and very understandable was the notion that wealth would be gained and there would be a triumphant return to the motherland with pockets full of money. The adults, mothers and fathers never doubted on the day of their departure from their native soil that one day in the not so distant future they would be leading their families like a Moses or an Aaron out of the bondage of north west European industrialised society with its ruthless Anglo Saxon work ethic back to their more easy going, Mediterranean promised land. The illusion was that they would return as the same people who had left, they and their children together, to reclaim their former lives with the difference that they would now have far more wealth, gained in distant lands where they had sacrificed a few years so that they could live more easily in their country. They would build houses, make suitable marriages for their children and have a better standard of life than their wealthy neighbours who had previously looked down upon them and who did not have to immigrate to improve their lives. They would live happily ever after, they thought and they dreamed. Alas, it was not to be.

Very few immigrants ever made the return journey. It might be difficult to make the decision to leave your country even when life is difficult but when you have done so and through hard work you have built a new home, made new relations, acquired a new language, where the death of old parents is mourned or marriage and the birth of a new generation is celebrated, then the thought of return begins to lack immediate importance and it is pushed further back in the order of priorities. Eventually, after many years the thought of the return is something vague and is treated with a lack of conviction that it would ever happen. Where else would you belong except in the place where destiny has brought you, the place where you worked and made a life for your self? Millions of people, like the waves of the sea, relentlessly moved from east to west or from north to south, heading towards centres of economic wealth and activity. People went to America, Australia, Western Europe in search of work and a better life. Was there ever a mass return to the old nests, back across the wide sea? No, there was not. Such an undertaking seemed too difficult, too uncomfortable. It was a one way journey. Yet, even people like myself who have grown from childhood into adulthood in England, in some nostalgic moments may feel that we are far from home and may yearn to return to an experience that is no longer there. Such thoughts are quickly dismissed as silly fantasies, which of course, they are.

There has been a very gradual metamorphosis. It now feels as if it happened in secret, perhaps while we slept, in the dark, unobserved. Actually this is not the case; it happened while we were wide awake and in fact, we all in our own distinctive way wanted to blend, to adopt and to facilitate the metamorphosis. One might ask, why not, it's a very natural reaction: change according to your environment or face extinction. I think that most people carry the instinct for survival in their genetic make up and anyway, the metamorphosis was very much a creative, positive process in which many individuals found the possibility to achieve their potential and for the Cypriot community in the UK to gain sense of identity that is different from the Cypriots of Cyprus.

At the beginning the alteration was no more then a thin, cosmetic veneer. The clothes that were brought in the suitcase, the suit made by the local village tailor, the dress made by the village seamstress or the shoes cobbled by the village shoemaker soon wore out and were eagerly replaced by English fabrics and London fashions. Clothes and hairstyles were the first obvious changes and they related to outward appearance and projection of the self. But there were deeper and more significant changes that had to be made quickly and were essential for the sake of immediate economic survival and eventual prosperity: the mothers and the fathers who had made the journey and had arrived here mostly penniless now entered the factories of England to make a beginning in the financial security of the their families. The rhythm of the day was determined by the clocking in and the clocking out at the factory entrance. The many religious holidays that had been enjoyed with festivities in the villages and towns of Cyprus were remembered but had to be mainly ignored except for those religious dates like Christmas and Easter that were shared with the British. There were also new words that had become permanent fixtures in the language of the new arrivals: "please", "thank you", "marketa", "buso". Appearance, manners and language had suddenly taken on a slightly different hue, shape, tone and texture.

Undoubtedly, the very fibre of our identity had begun to change but so gradual was it that it was hardly noticed by those who were experiencing it. The change gathered momentum and it is still moving on. For us, the children who have been raised in England or who were born here, the experience of the migration lives on vaguely like a dream. We see ourselves as children holding our parents by the hand leaving our troubled, fractured land behind in search of a new home, far away in a distant country. This is the experience that the immigrant never forgets; the day of the departure from his home land, the journey and finally reaching his destination from which he imagines that one day he will return to find the place and the people that he had once left behind, not realising that the human condition is always in a state of change and that nowhere and no group of people or individual ever remains the same.

We, who crossed the ocean, underwent the metamorphosis that still continues. On this new stage, we played our part according to the scene and action of a different kind of play that is called England. Those, who were left behind, also changed according to the circumstances that befell them. They had to face 1974 with all its tragic consequences. Our experiences were quite different so that now we feel more strongly the distance of geography, events and the passing of time. And now, who are we? What are we? For our parents there were changes but they were not so deep and they held onto their often unrealised and unreal dreams of the return. But for us who were brought here as babies or were born here and our children and grandchildren, because the generations role on unceasingly, how have we fared?

We have become a part of the scene; we have blended almost fully but not entirely. It is not a matter of choice, a decision that is made, but rather it is a part of an evolutionary process, a kind of dialectic that brings new realities into being.

The synthesis for the Cypriot community is not yet complete. We are still caught up in the in between period. In my opinion, British people have always tried to be fair to the immigrants who have arrived at these shores and we, the immigrants, have found safety, security and the opportunity to pursue and fulfil our goals in life. Yet, we still do not feel that we are entirely a part of the main; there is the feeling that we remain as islands surrounded by a beneficent British ocean whose waves gently massage our coastline. Perhaps, the umbilical cord with the old mother country is still attached to our hearts so that even for those of us who grew up in England or even for those who were born here, we cannot forget the roots of our origins. This can be seen by how devastated British Cypriots felt when in 1974 the Turkish army invaded Cyprus and murdered many ordinary people and effectively partitioned the island. British Cypriots organized themselves to offer whatever help they could to their unfortunate brethren on the island. I suppose this suggests that though our identity must belong to our present experience, our past has also an unforgettable and important bearing on our understanding of who we are.

The Tourist

Returning to Cyprus for me is always a special event and a journey which is always more than just a package holiday. At such times, I find myself thinking back to that life changing outward journey from Cyprus to England that I made as a little boy so many years before. I remember that day very distinctly: my hand was tightly gripped by my mother as if I could somehow disappear from the face of the earth if she held my hand more loosely. I was excited that we were going to board a huge ship, the type that I had watched from the beach at Varosi, steaming by in the distance with black smoke churning out of its funnels. Boarding the ship was indeed a day of immense excitement like the days when we went to the panayiri at Sotira or Stylloi and would stay with grandmother or one of our aunties.

After we had boarded the ship there was no return to the world that we had left behind; it changed beyond recognition and even to this day if we travel to Cyprus , the return to Varosi, our home town, itself remains elusive and beyond possibility. We can only look on from afar with sadness and nostalgia at the city that has become a ghost, which only has life in our memories and the hope in our hearts that one day the barbed wire and the illegal occupation will come to an end.

There is also the memory of the grandmother whose tears and anguish could not be hidden or disguised on the day of our departure while grandfather sadly and silently looked at the ground. We would never see them again.

When we visit Cyprus for our holidays, I instinctively look for familiar places or familiar faces that might somehow connect to the life before our exodus. There are thankfully some surviving aunts and uncles who have been blessed with good health and long life and whom I am always overjoyed to see again.

The saddest feature from the past is for me the sight of the ghost city of Varosi; it is lifeless and empty while the people of Cyprus wait in anticipation for the day of its resurrection. But Cyprus, despite all its endless political problems, despite the ghost city, has become modern, courageous and daring, full of talented, skilful and enterprising young people hungry for success.

During our brief holidays on the island we might be searching for a past and the people there often kindly tolerate our eccentricities because they know us and the background to our quests. A certain feeling or emotion that I experience whenever I return to Cyprus is that when I come out from arrivals at Larnaca Airport, I quite irrationally expect some kind of a welcome home reception but there is no one their except the faces of strangers. The friends, the uncles and aunts with their hoards of children who made such a noise, the sweet grandmother who wept to see us go on the day of our exodus and the grandfather with the sad down cast expression but with the big heart full of love are not there to renew the bonds that once held us together. There is a price that is paid for seeking a better life beyond one's native shores. At some point the bonds between the old life and the new are surely and inevitably cut. The umbilical cord cannot hold forever.

We now return as tourists to what was once the place where we lived and where if not for the decision to leave, our lives would have been totally different. When I arrive with my family we are picked up by a taxi or sometimes there is a coach and we are taken to our hotel. This is all rather well organised and we are pleased with the efficiency of the locals. On most occasions when we arrive at the hotel we are further satisfied with the clean, comfortable rooms with the sea view. During these episodes in Cyprus, I try not to show that I am not just a tourist but that I am also a local boy because it is usually apparent that we are from elsewhere particularly through our clumsy use of the Greek language. In hearing our spoken Greek usage or observing our futile attempts to appear as natives, the locals might be provoked into a gentle laughter that stems from the genuine humour of the circumstances and in most cases it is meant with sympathy and kindness.

My visits to Cyprus always invoke in me thoughts not only about my early childhood and about the people who were left behind but also about my life in the UK. This probably happens because on holiday one has the time of day to think and reflect about our past. Inevitably, I find that very often my mind wanders back to events which I suppose were the most important for me in my personal development. Thoughts of my school days, during which I was inspired by my wonderful teachers to learn to love the English Language and its great wealth of literature, come flooding back to me. This success at school enabled me to attend university and then to become a teacher. I remember my father saying that it was his greatest pride that he had a son who had graduated from university and had become a teacher. He would sometimes say to me:

"Fotaki, it is a great and noble achievement to be a teacher because you are entrusted with the future of the younger generation. In my village", he would continue speaking in a fond and gentle manner when ever reminiscing about pleasant memories from the past, "in my village the teacher was greatly respected. The village people with children at school always took him presents for Christmas and Easter. They gave him a freshly slaughtered chicken, some halloumia and dried, rolled trahana for making soup. In the summer the teacher's presents were fresh fruit and vegetables. When ever he entered the kafenion he was quickly offered a chair immediately and a dozen men insisted on paying for his coffee. Yes, the teacher is always greatly respected."

When ever he thought about the past, he would stare silently in the space in front of him for a moment or two, as if evoking the picture of the memory in his mind. When satisfied he would focus his eyes on the present, smile and continue his conversation. I suppose he had some romantic notion regarding the lives of teachers. He was speaking of another place and another time. Little did he realise just how difficult the lives of teachers in London could be! Even in Cyprus, society has changed so much that my father's experience of school and the respect for teachers is today something very different from what he remembered and described. Mothers, fathers, sisters, brothers, grandmothers, grandfathers, wives and husbands, the list of people we have known stretches from our birth to our present. We evoke the images of the people who we have known, the people whom we love and sometimes the people who have caused us pain or discomfort. We hear their voices from the past speaking clearly and audibly as if they are never far away, as if they are speaking to us here and now.

~

As I sit under the canopy of a beach cafe looking out at the turquoise blue Mediterranean Sea, the realisation manifests itself more clearly than perhaps the previous year that this patch work of experiences that seem to have been woven together in slow motion equal an important part of my life time and have given my personality form and shape. My experiences have defined my identity as both not quite a Cypriot nor entirely British but a synthesis of the two. I am truly what Cypriots now call the people who immigrated to England, I am an Englezokypraios. Sometimes this feels like an awkward position to be in but most of the time I and others like me are happy and comfortable with our identity and who we have become as a result of having spent our lives in England. The question of identity is no longer an issue, neither for us nor for the people of the United Kingdom with whom we have made our lives. We simply just get on with our every day affairs without any longer thinking that the stage is in England and that we are somehow in the wrong kind of drama. In fact, our new roles in our new land feel very natural. It has taken many years to arrive at this new sense of identity and we now understand that identity is not only the memory of a history, it is also the feeling of a natural interaction with your present environment and the sense that you belong to it more than to any other place.

This sense of belonging can manifest itself in many ways but for me it is through an attachment to a particular scene or place. One such experience is when after some visit abroad, our aeroplane begins to descend over the Home Counties revealing the rolling hills of southern England, sometimes basking in sunshine, with lush green fields divided with hedge groves in unparalleled neatness. This scene always prompts me to think that while other places have beauty, the beauty of England is indeed unique. Another example of the sentimental feelings that I have for England is my passionate love for London. One of my favourite places in London is Parliament Hill, near Highgate. When on occasion I happen to visit this location, as I stand at the summit of the hill on a clear day, looking across the panorama of this vast, majestic city, picking out the familiar land marks of Saint Paul's Cathedral, Big Ben, The Post Office Tower and further east, the buildings of Canary Wharf confidently thrusting their towers into the skyline, I sense the dynamic vitality of this great beating heart that I first felt as a little boy who journeyed here from far away and which I now call my home.

~

Bibliography /other sources.

1. Enoch Powell's "Rivers of Blood" speech.
   www.martinfrost.ws/htmlfiles/rivers-blood2.html.-United States.

2. Gallop poll.
   en.metapedia.org/wiki/Enoch-Powell

3. "Strong meat"
   en.wikipedia.org/wiki/Rivers-of-Blood-Speech